PETRIFIED FOREST
NATIONAL PARK
ACTIVITY BOOK

PUZZLES, MAZES, GAMES, AND MORE ABOUT PETRIFIED FOREST NATIONAL PARK

NATIONAL PARKS ACTIVITIES SERIES

PETRIFIED FOREST NATIONAL PARK
ACTIVITY BOOK

Copyright 2022
Published by Little Bison Press

The author acknowledges that the land on which Petrified Forest National Park is located are the traditional lands of the Diné Bikéyah, Pueblos, Zuni, and Hopi peoples.

LITTLE BISON
Press

For more free national parks activities, visit
www.littlebisonpress.com

About Petrified Forest National Park

Petrified Forest National Park is located in the state of Arizona. The park's namesake is the abundant and colorful pieces of petrified wood that can be found throughout the park. While walking in the park you can see a forest that looks very different than you might expect. While Petrified Forest has some living trees, most of the trees you'll see in this "forest" don't really look like trees at all. The trees you'll see here are petrified, which means they were turned to stone over time.

Part of Historic Route 66 runs through Petrified Forest, the only national park with a section of this significant piece of American history. Travelers of today can experience what it was like for travelers of yesteryear. Although the Painted Desert Inn no longer offers lodging, you can explore a museum and see where people of the past rested, played, and dined.

You can also see other rock formations called mesas, buttes, and hoodoos that are caused by the wind and rain.

Petrified Forest National Park is famous for:
- rainbow colored hills
- desert wildlife
- fossils

Hey, I'm Parker!

I'm the only snail in history to visit every National Park in the United States! Come join me on my adventures in Petrified Forest National Park.

Throughout this book, we will learn about the history of the park, the animals and plants that live here, and things to do if you ever visit in person. This book is also full of games and activities!

Last but not least, I am hidden 9 times on different pages. See how many times you can find me. This page doesn't count!

Petrified Forest Bingo

Let's play bingo! Cross off each box you are able to during your visit to the national park. Try to get a bingo down, across, or diagonally. If you can't visit the park, use the bingo board to plan your perfect trip.

Pick out some activities you would want to do during your visit. What would you do first? How long would you spend there? What animals would you try to see?

SPOT A PRONGHORN	SEE THE PAINTED DESERT	GO FOR A HIKE	TAKE A PICTURE AT AN OVERLOOK	WATCH A MOVIE AT THE VISITORS CENTER
IDENTIFY A TREE	LEARN ABOUT THE INDIGENOUS PEOPLE WHO LIVE IN THIS AREA	WITNESS A SUNRISE OR SUNSET	OBSERVE THE NIGHT SKIES	VISIT THE FOSSILS AT THE DEMO LAB
HEAR A BIRD CALL	SPOT A BUTTE OR MESA	FREE SPACE	WALK AROUND THE PAINTED DESERT INN	SPOT SOME ANIMAL TRACKS
PICK UP TEN PIECES OF TRASH	HAVE A PICNIC	SEE SOME PETROGLYPHS	VISIT THE AGATE HOUSE	SPOT A BIRD OF PREY
LEARN ABOUT THE HISTORY OF ROUTE 66	OBSERVE SOME PETRIFIED WOOD	GO CAMPING	VISIT A RANGER STATION	PARTICIPATE IN A RANGER-LED ACTIVITY

Color the Petrified Wood

Petrified Forest National Park is home to fossils from plants and animals that lived many years ago. Petrified wood is a tree fossil. Over hundreds and thousands of years, minerals replaced the organic materials in the wood. As a result, petrified wood is much heavier than regular wood.

Take a Hike

Go for a hike with your friends or family. If you aren't able to visit Petrified Forest National Park, go for a walk in a park near where you live. Read through the prompts before your walk and finish the activities after you return.

Draw something you saw that moves:

Draw something you saw when you looked up:

Draw something you saw that grows out of the ground:

Draw a picture of your favorite part of the walk:

Draw a Barn Owl

Complete the picture below by drawing the other half of the owl. Finish the image by coloring it in.

Barn owls have excellent hearing that allows them to hunt in the dark. They are predators of small animals like mice and other small rodents. Great horned owls will harass or hunt barn owls.

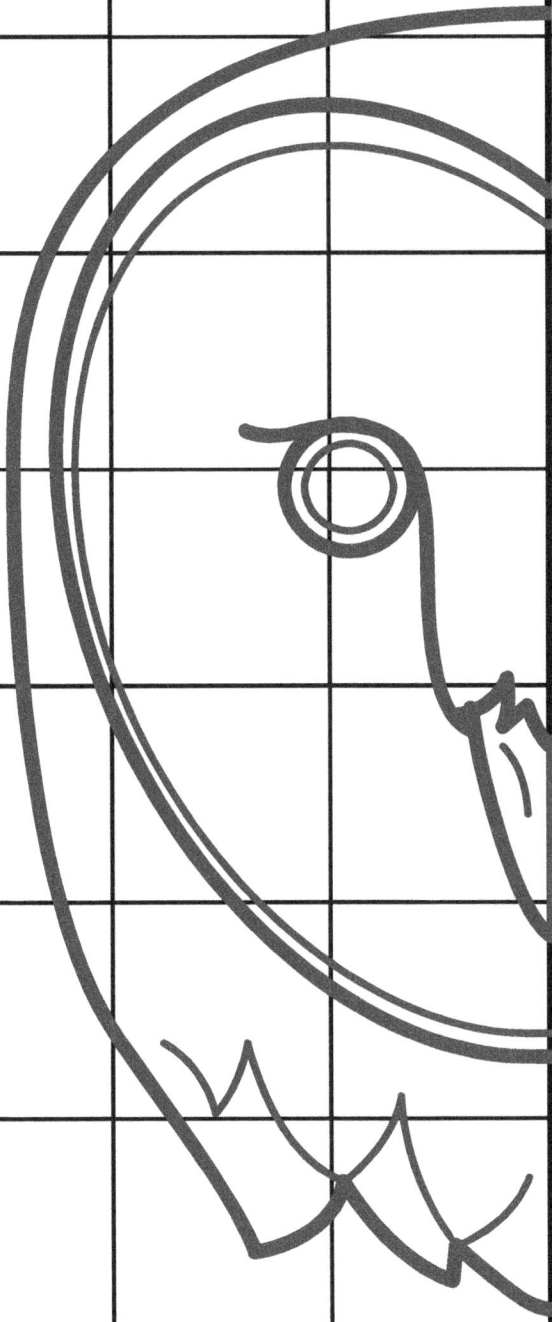

Go Horseback Riding in the Painted Desert

Help find the horse's lost shoe!

start here →

Camping Packing List

What should you take with you when you go camping? Pretend you are in charge of your family camping trip. Make a list of what you would need to be safe and comfortable on an overnight excursion. Some considerations are listed on the side.

1.
2.
3.
4.
5.
6.
7.
8.
9.
10.
11.
12.
13.
14.
15.
16.

- What will you eat at every meal?

- What will the weather be like?

- Where will you sleep?

- What will you do during your free time?

- How luxurious do you want your camp to be?

- How will you cook?

- How will you see at night?

- How will you dispose of trash?

- What might you need in case of emergencies?

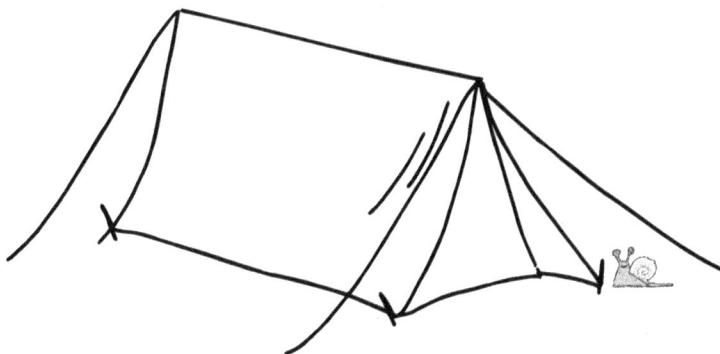

Petrified Forest National Park

Date: _____

Season: _____

Who I went with: _____

Which entrance: _____

How was your experience? Write a few sentences about your trip. Where did you stay? What did you do? What was your favorite activity? If you haven't visited the park yet, write a paragraph pretending that you did.

_____

_____

_____

_____

_____

_____

STAMPS

Many national parks and monuments have cancellation stamps for visitors to use. These rubber stamps record the date and location that you visited. Many people collect the markings as a free souvenir. Check with a ranger to see where you can find a stamp during your visit. If you aren't able to find one, you can draw your own.

Where is the Park?

Petrified Forest National Park is in the southwestern United States. It is located in Arizona, 50 miles from the border of New Mexico. Arizona is home to two other national parks, Saguaro National Park and Grand Canyon National Park.

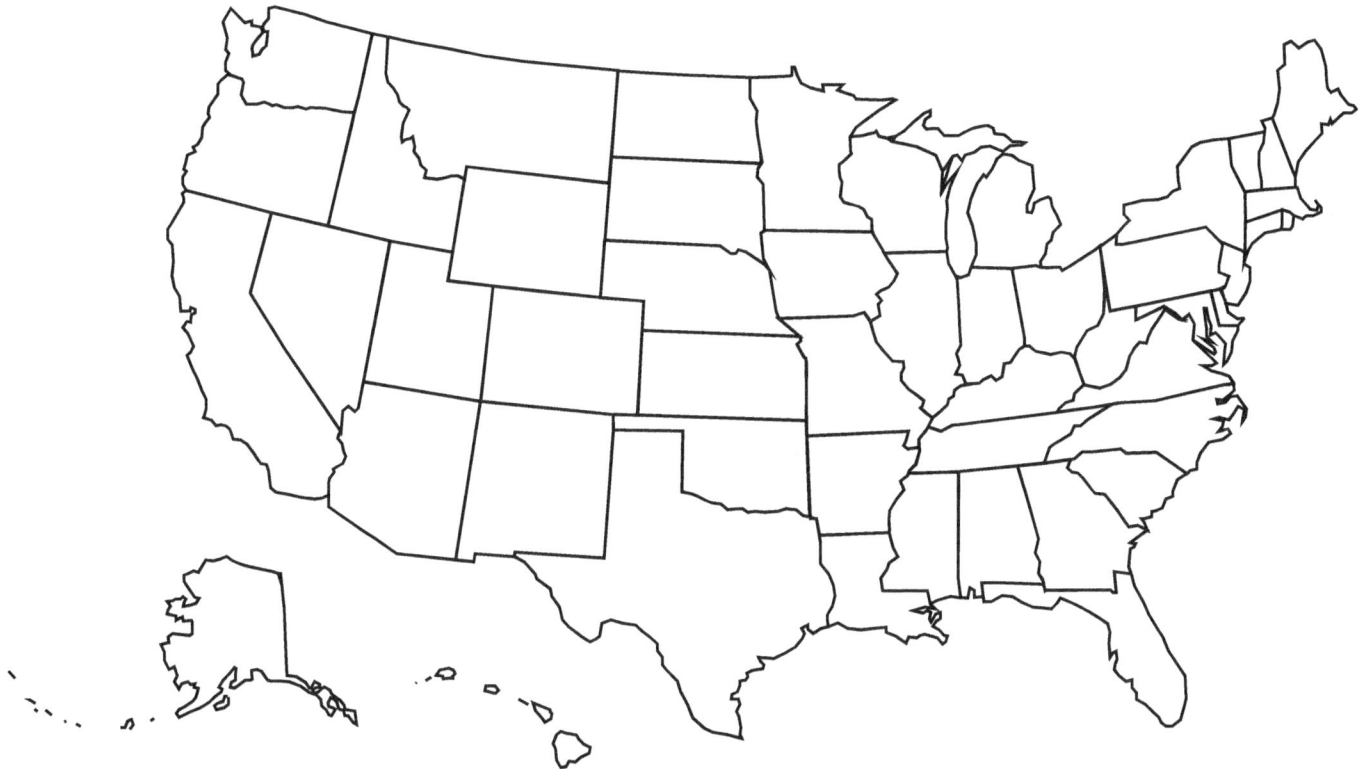

Arizona

Look at the shape of Arizona. Can you find it on the map? If you are from the US, can you find your home state? Color Arizona red. Put a star on the map where you live.

The Beautiful Badlands 🔍

People come from all over the world to check out the unique layers of the badlands at Petrified Forest Park. If you are able to see the badlands for yourself, make some observations.

Draw or describe them in the boxes below, using lots of detail.

Something colorful	A unique rock	Something that moves
An insect	Something cool you saw	A tiny plant
Something with a smell	A leaf	Something shiny

Exploring the Dark Sky

This park is a popular destination for stargazing. You may see stars in the night sky here that you may not see at home. Why do you think that is?

For all of time, people from across the world have looked at the night sky and seen images in the stars. They created stories about groups of stars, also called constellations. Create your own constellation that you see in the starfield below!

What is your constellation named?

Who Lives in Petrified Forest?

Below are 7 plants and animals that live in the park. Use the word bank to fill in the clues below. Pay attention to how many letters each word has to see where it fits.

☐☐☐☐ A ☐

☐☐☐☐☐☐ R ☐☐☐

☐ I ☐ ■ ☐☐☐

☐☐☐ Z ☐☐☐

☐☐☐☐ O ☐☐☐☐☐

☐☐☐ N ☐☐☐☐☐

☐ A ☐☐☐☐☐☐☐☐

WORD BANK: COTTONWOOD, PRONGHORN, SALAMANDER, BOBCAT, BURROGRASS, KIT FOX, BUZZARD

14

Animals of Petrified Forest National Park

Badgers
are a member of the weasel family and dig their burrows with their huge front claws.

Great Plains Toads
can be identified by their pale green color with dark green spots.

Striped Skunks
are known for their stinky defense mechanism.

Greater Short-horned Lizards can squirt blood from their eyes to deter predators from eating them.

Barn Owls have asymmetrical ears, allowing them to hear better to hunt.

Common Names
vs.
Scientific Names

A common name of an organism is a name that is based on everyday language. You have heard the common names of plants, animals, and other living things on tv, in books, and at school. Common names can also be referred to as "English" names, popular names, or farmer's names. Common names can vary from place to place. The word for a particular tree may be one thing, but that same tree has a different name in another country. Common names can even vary from region to region, even in the same country.

Scientific names, or Latin names, are given to organisms to make it possible to have uniform names for the same species. Scientific names are in Latin. You may have heard plants or animals referred to by their scientific name or parts of their scientific names. Latin names are also called "binomial nomenclature," which refers to a two-part naming system. The first part of the name – the generic name – refers to the genus to which the species belongs. The second part of the name, the specific name, identifies the species. For example, Tyrannosaurus rex is an example of a widely known scientific name.

Coyote

Canis latrans

COMMON NAME

Brewer's Blackbird

Euphagus cyanocephalus

LATIN NAME = GENUS + SPECIES
Coyote = Canis latrans
Brewer's Blackbird = Euphagus cyanocephalus

16

Find the Match!
Common Names and Latin Names

Match the common name to the scientific name for each animal. The first one is done for you. Use clues on the page before and after this one to complete the matches.

Striped Skunk	Haliaeetus leucocephalus
Coyote	Peromyscus maniculatus
Starvation Prickly Pear	Pinus edulis
Deer Mouse	Cynomys gunnisoni
Great Horned Owl	Canis latrans
Bald Eagle	Yucca baccata
Piñon Pine	Bubo virginianus
Gunnison's Prairie Dog	Mephitis mephitis
Banana Yucca	Opuntia polyacantha

Bald Eagle
Haliaeetus leucocephalus

Deer Mouse
Peromyscus maniculatus

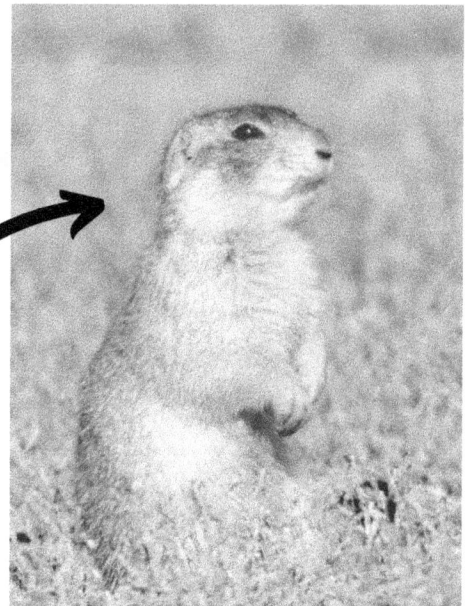

Gunnison's prairie dog
Cynomys gunnisoni

Great Horned Owl
Bubo virginianus

Some plants and animals that live in Petrified Forest

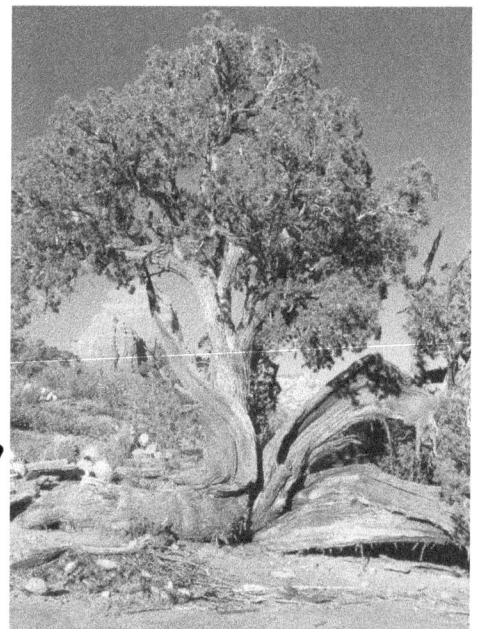

Piñon Pine
Pinus edulis

Starvation Prickly Pear
Opuntia polyacantha

Banana Yucca
Yucca baccata

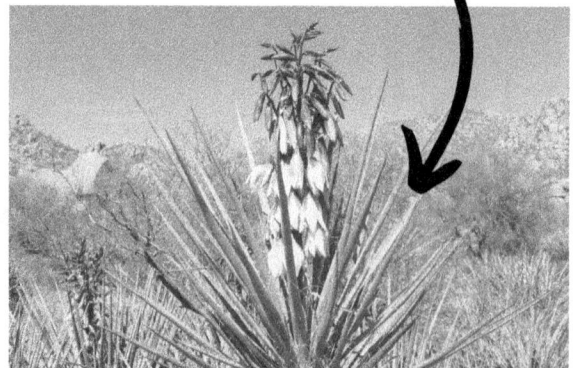

Things To Do Jumble

Unscramble the letters to uncover activities you can do while in Petrified Forest National Park. Hint: each one ends in -ing.

1. CAGEOCH ☐☐☐☐☐☐☐ING

2. IHK ☐☐☐ING

3. DBIR ☐☐☐☐ING

4. MACP ☐☐☐☐ING

5. KINICPC ☐☐☐☐☐☐☐ING

6. EISSTEHG ☐☐☐☐☐☐☐☐ING

7. SARTGZA ☐☐☐☐☐☐☐ING

Word Bank

birding
reading
camping
stargazing
horseback riding
hiking
swimming
singing
geocaching
sightseeing
picnicking

19

Prairie Dog Digs

Prairie dog colonies, or "towns," are made up of tunnels that are 3 to 6 feet below ground and about 15 feet long. These burrows usually include several distinct chambers inhabited by a coterie, or group, of prairie dogs. These coteries work together to protect the group from predators such as coyotes, badgers, birds of prey, and bobcats. Prairie dog burrows have areas dug out for raising babies, sleeping, and even toilets. They also feature dugouts near the exits, so the prairie dogs can listen to potential predators outside.

Using your knowledge of prairie dog habitat, draw your own version of a prairie dog burrow. Your drawing should include at least 3 different chambers, a coterie with at least 4 prairie dogs, and one potential predator waiting on the surface.

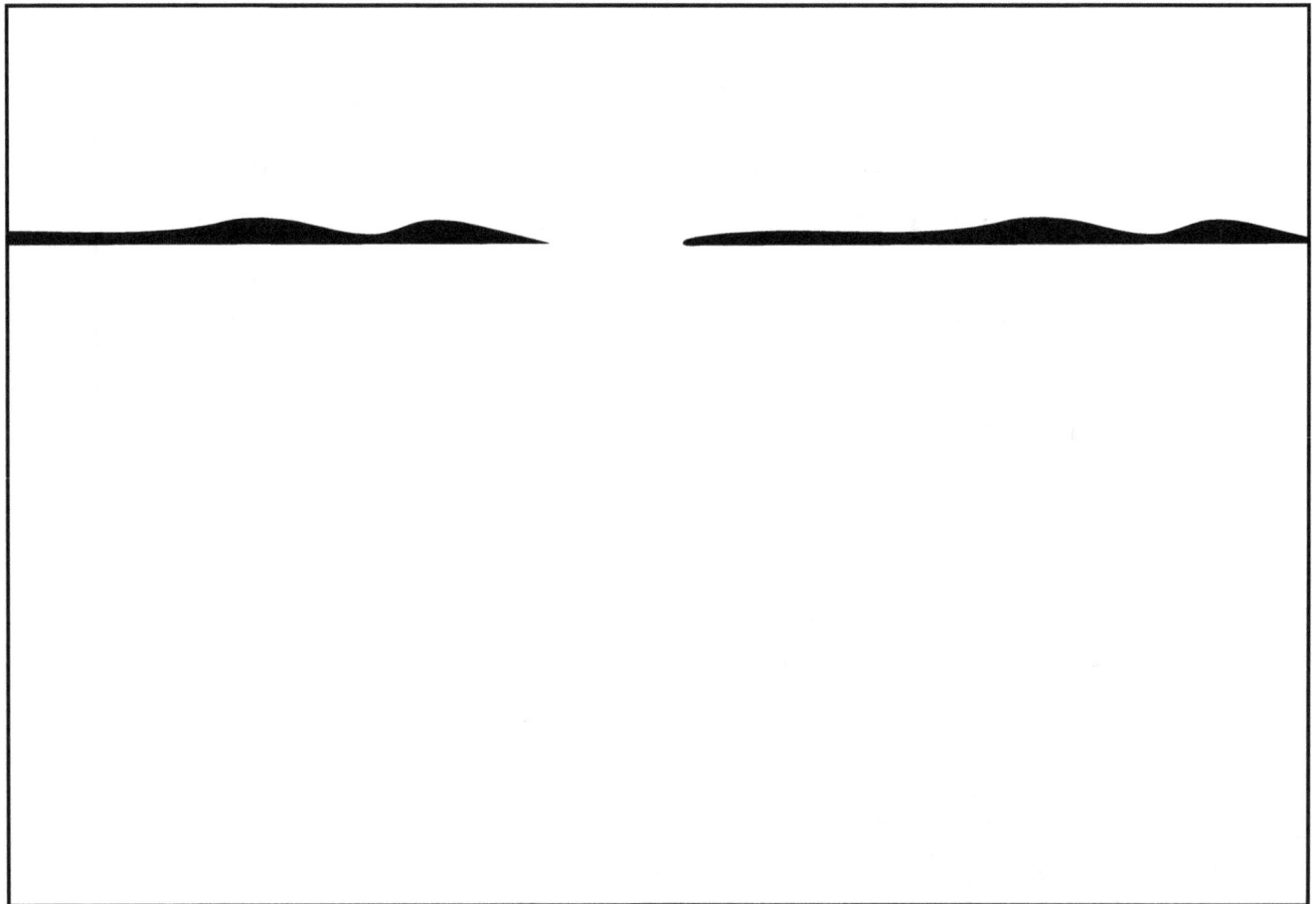

Which predator of the prairie dog did you draw? Do you think it will be able to successfully hunt any members of your coterie?

_____

_____

_____

Sound Exploration

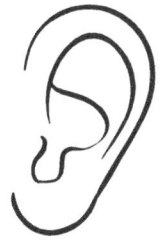

Spend a minute or two listening to all of the sounds around you.
Draw your favorite sound.

How did this sound make you feel?

_____

_____

What did you think when you heard this sound?

_____

_____

The National Park Logo

The National Park System has over 400 units in the US. Just like Petrified Forest National Park, each location is unique or special in some way. The areas include other national parks, historic sites, monuments, seashores, and other recreation areas.

Each element of the National Park emblem represents something that the National Park Service protects. Fill in each blank below to show what each symbol represents.

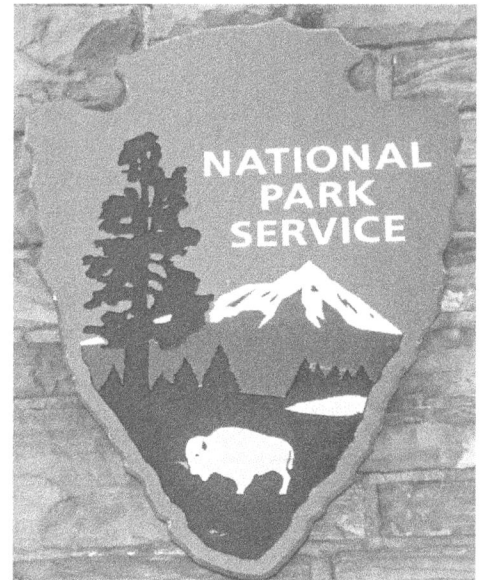

```
WORD BANK:
_____
MOUNTAINS, ARROWHEAD, BISON,
SEQUOIA TREE, WATER
```

This represents all plants: _____

This represents all animals: _____

This represents the landscapes: _____

This represents the waters protected by the park service: _____

This represents the historical and archeological values: _____

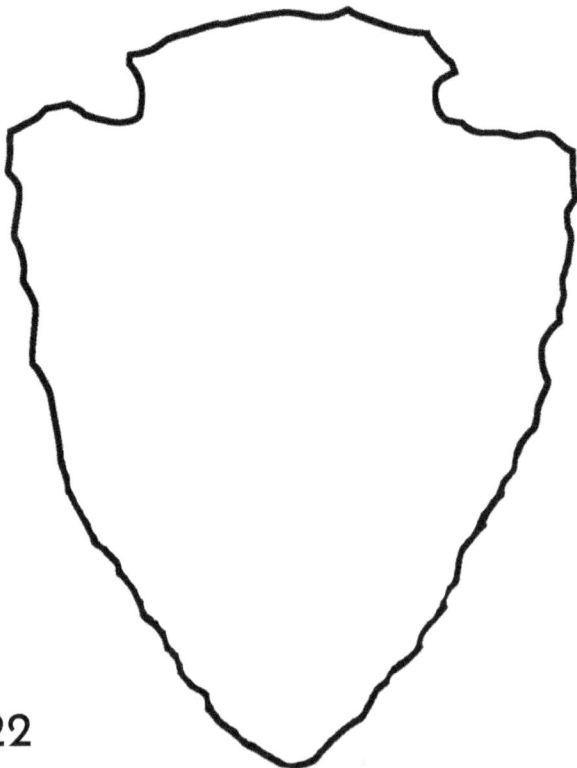

Now it's your turn! Pretend you are designing a new national park. Add elements to the design that represent the things your park protects.

What is the name of your park?

Describe why you included the symbols that you chose. What do they mean?

The Ten Essentials

Careful preparation and knowledge are key to a successful adventure into Petrified Forest's backcountry.

The ten essentials are a list of things that are important to have when you go for longer hikes. If you go on a hike to the <u>backcountry</u>, it is especially important that you have everything you need in case of an emergency. If you get lost or something unforeseen happens, it is good to be prepared to survive until help finds you.

The ten essentials list was developed in the 1930s by an outdoors group called the Mountaineers. Over time and technological advancements, this list has evolved. Can you identify all the things on the current list? Circle each of the "essentials" and cross out everything that doesn't make the cut.

fire: matches, lighter, tinder, and/or stove	a pint of milk	extra money	headlamp, plus extra batteries	extra clothes
extra water	a dog	Polaroid camera	bug net	lightweight games, like a deck of cards
extra food	a roll of duct tape	shelter	sun protection, such as sunglasses, sun-protective clothes, and sunscreen	knife, plus a gear repair kit
a mirror	navigation: map, compass, altimeter, GPS device, or satellite messenger	first aid kit	extra flip-flops	entertainment, such as video games or books

Backcountry - a remote, undeveloped rural area.

Design a Set of Stickers

Imagine you have been hired to design a sticker set that will be for sale in the national park gift shop. These stickers will be a souvenir for visitors to put on water bottles, notebooks, laptops, and more.

You could include a plant or animal that lives here, the park name and the year it was established, or a famous place in the park or activity that you can do while visiting. Make sure to use colors that you think represent the park!

Petrified Forest Word Search

Words may be horizontal, vertical, or diagonal
and they might be backward!

1. TREES
2. BADLANDS
3. PUERCO
4. PUEBLO
5. LONG LOGS
6. PALEONTOLOGY
7. PAINTED
8. HOPI
9. ZUNI
10. NAVAJO
11. TIME
12. BASKETMAKER
13. HOLBROOK
14. PETRIFIED
15. ARIZONA
16. FOSSIL
17. AGATE HOUSE

```
C W P A L E O N T O L O G Y K
H T U P K I A I C R E L A N P
T G E O U O M R C C E B A R E
P M R A Y E R S I E R L I E T
I I C D R A B L O Z I P I K R
N F O S S I L L D C O T K A I
Y E S E E H E K O H P N I M F
S G O L G N O L G E N E A T I
N E H B S D T O R E C D G E E
E C I C A D T U S H P I O K D
I K A P A I N T E D K E T S N
N R O A K O E A O V O K I A E
E I P O T Z D E L E R T L B W
J C G F R O U E P D O R V E H
Z I L S E B I N A V A J O E A
U T A I E E L G E Z E B R N L
N T D T S E N O Y N A C C I E
I J U O E S U O H E T A G A Z
```

Wildlife Wisdom

The national park is home to many different kinds of animals. Seeing wildlife can be an exciting part of visiting the national park but it is important to remember that these animals are wild. They need plenty of space and a healthy habitat where they can find their own food. Part of this is not allowing animals to eat any human food. This is their home and we are the visitors. We need to be respectful of the wildlife in the park.

Directions: Circle the highlighted words that best complete the following sentences.

If an animal changes its behavior because of your presence, you are:
A) too close
B) funny looking
C) dehydrated and should drink more water

The best thing we can do to help wild animals survive is:
A) make them pets
B) protect their habitat
C) knit them winter sweaters

In a national park, it is okay to share your food with wild animals:
A) never
B) always
C) sometimes

When you're hiking in an area where there are bears, you should warn bears that you are entering their space by:
A) hiking quietly
B) making noise
C) wearing bright colors

At night, park rangers care for the animals by:
A) putting them back into their cages
B) tucking them into bed
C) leaving them alone

If you see an abandoned bird's nest, it is best to:
A) pet the baby birds
B) leave it alone
C) crunch the empty eggshells

Rock squirrels look in bushes in hopes of finding:
A) granola bars
B) leaves, stems, and seeds
C) peanuts to eat

The place where an animal lives is called its:
A) condo
B) habitat
C) crib

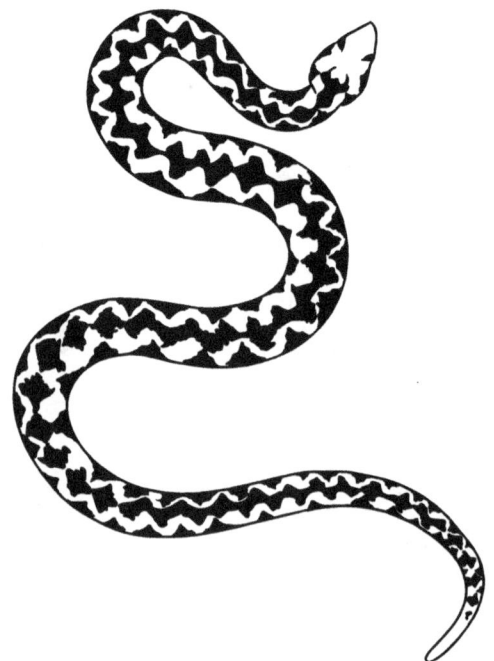

Connect the Dots

Connect the dots to figure out what this tiny critter is. There are six types of these that live in Petrified Forest National Park.

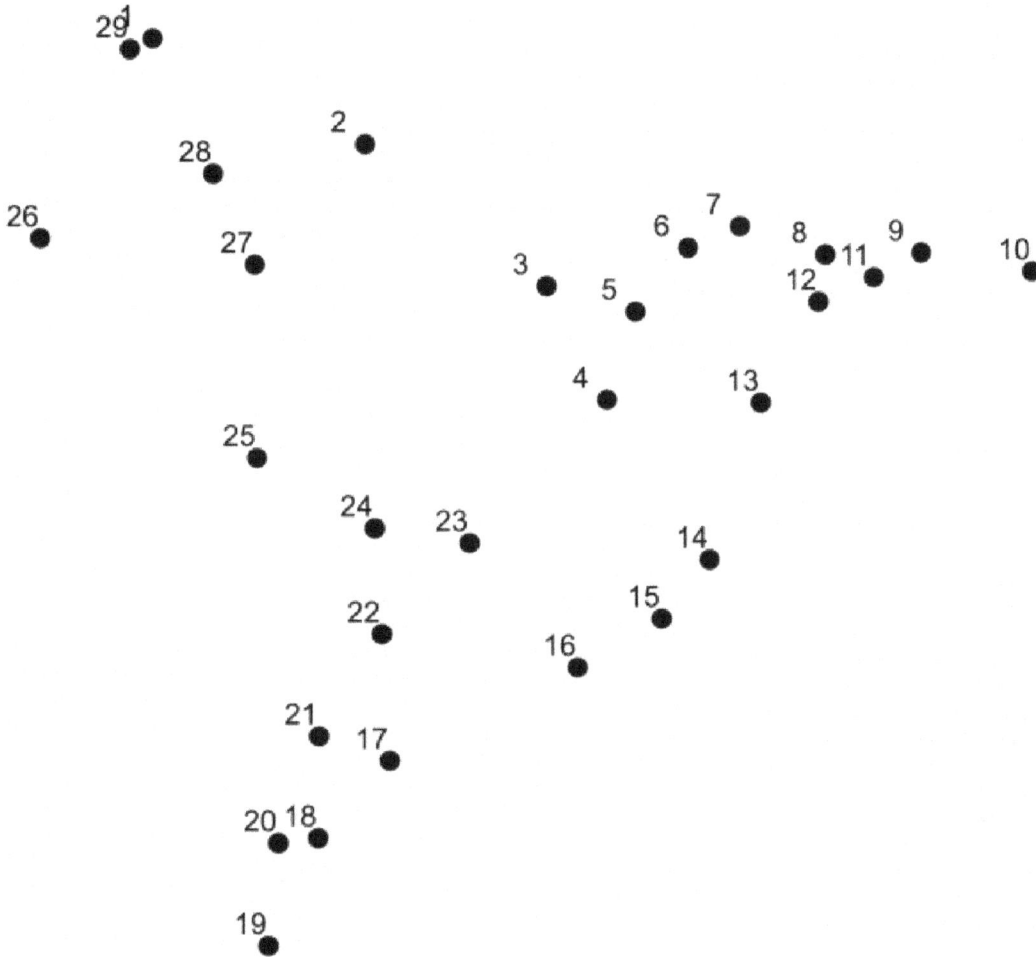

29 1
2
28
26
27
7
6
8 9
3 11 10
5 12
4 13
25
24 23
14
15
22
16
21
17
20 18
19

Their heart rate can reach as high as 1,260 beats per minute and a breathing rate of 250 breaths per minute. Have you ever measured your breathing rate? Ask a friend or family member to set a timer for 60 seconds. Once they say "go," try to breathe normally. Count each breath until they say "stop." How do your breaths per minute compare to hummingbirds?

_____

_____

The Perfect Picnic Spot

Fill in the blanks on this page without looking at the full story. Once you have each line filled out, use the words you've chosen to complete the story on the next page.

EMOTION _____

FOOD _____

SOMETHING SWEET _____

STORE _____

MODE OF TRANSPORTATION _____

NOUN _____

SOMETHING ALIVE _____

SAUCE _____

PLURAL VEGETABLES _____

ADJECTIVE _____

PLURAL BODY PART _____

ANIMAL _____

PLURAL FRUIT _____

PLACE _____

SOMETHING TALL _____

COLOR _____

ADJECTIVE _____

NOUN _____

A DIFFERENT ANIMAL _____

FAMILY MEMBER #1 _____

FAMILY MEMBER #2 _____

VERB THAT ENDS IN -ING _____

A DIFFERENT FOOD _____

The Perfect Picnic Spot

Use the words from the previous page to complete a silly story.

When my family suggested having our lunch at the Chinde Point picnic area, I

was _ _ _ _ _ _ _ _. I love eating my _ _ _ _ _ _ outside! I knew we had picked up a
___EMOTION___ ___FOOD___

box of _ _ _ _ _ _ from the _ _ _ _ _ _ _ _ for after lunch, my favorite. We drove up
___SOMETHING SWEET___ ___STORE___

to the area and I jumped out of the _ _ _ _ _ _ _ _ _. "I will find the perfect spot for
___MODE OF TRANSPORTATION___

a picnic!" I grabbed a _ _ _ _ _ _ for us to sit on, and I ran off. I passed a picnic
___NOUN___

table, but it was covered with _ _ _ _ _ _ _ _ so we couldn't sit there. The next
___SOMETHING ALIVE___

picnic table looked okay, but there were smears of _ _ _ _ _ _ _ and pieces of
___SAUCE___

_ _ _ _ _ _ _ _ everywhere. The people that were there before must have been
___PLURAL VEGETABLES___

_ _ _ _ _ _! I gritted my _ _ _ _ _ _ _ together and kept walking down the path,
___ADJECTIVE___ ___PLURAL BODY PART___

determined to find the perfect spot. I wanted a table with a good view of the

hills. Why was this so hard? If we were lucky, I might even get to see _ _ _ _ _ _
___ANIMAL___

eating some _ _ _ _ _ _ on the cliffside. They don't have those in _ _ _ _ _ _ _, where
___PLURAL FRUIT___ ___PLACE___

I am from. I walked down a little hill and there it was, the perfect spot! The

shrubs towered overhead and looked as tall as _ _ _ _ _ _ _ _. The patch of plants
___SOMETHING TALL___

was a beautiful _ _ _ _ _ _ _ color. The _ _ _ _ _ _ flowers were growing on
___COLOR___ ___ADJECTIVE___

the side of a _ _ _ _ _ _ _. I looked across the hill's edge and even saw a
___NOUN___

_ _ _ _ _ _ _ _ on the edge of a rock. I looked back to see my _ _ _ _ _ _ _ _ _ and
___DIFFERENT ANIMAL___ ___FAMILY MEMBER #1___

_ _ _ _ _ _ _ _ _ _ _ _ _ _ _ _ a picnic basket. "I hope you brought plenty of
___FAMILY MEMBER #2___ ___VERB THAT ENDS IN ING___

_ _ _ _ _ _ _ _, I'm starving!"
___A DIFFERENT FOOD___

29

Hike to Hoodoos

start here →

Painted Desert Inn
Word Search

Once a place to rest for travelers on Route 66, the Painted Desert Inn is now a museum. If you visit the building today, you can learn about its history and see where tourists would eat, sleep, and admire the landscape of this area.

1. TREEHOUSE
2. LODGING
3. LORE
4. TOURIST
5. ROOM
6. CLAY
7. PUEBLO
8. STUCCO
9. STRUCTURE
10. HISTORIC
11. SOUVENIR
12. KABOTIE
13. MURAL
14. COLTER
15. LANDMARK
16. ICE CREAM
17. FLAGSTONE

```
P K A B O T I E A Y I D E O W
G N I G D O L M A T I O N R O
T V D T C U L E L W A L K O T
S E U C S R E G A O T T B M H
G E U L O I O C R E R R S K M
M T D L Y S R O U R E E L O A
S O S E H T C R M O E R L E E
A R B S I K I B D I H T O M R
L S A O S I L O E O O D L P C
L L I D T R K N K E U G B O E
F K A C O T I I N L S B E O C
S R L S R A O C S A E K U R I
T A O T I H I N Z I I L P E C
Y M A R C O O W K C O R D E B
R D R A S T R U C T U R E E M
T N E W G R E E E L B R T M T
L A D G E R I N E V U O S E B
F L A G S T O N E H Y S G O N
```

Leave No Trace Quiz

Leave No Trace is a concept that helps people make decisions during outdoor recreation that protects the environment. There are seven principles that guide us when we spend time outdoors, whether you are in a national park or not. Are you an expert in Leave No Trace? Take this quiz and find out!

1. How can you plan ahead and prepare to ensure you have the best experience you can in the national park?
   a. Make sure you stop by the ranger station for a map and to ask about current conditions.
   b. Just wing it! You will know the best trail when you see it.
   c. Stick to your plan, even if conditions change. You traveled a long way to get here, and you should stick to your plan.
2. What is an example of traveling on a durable surface?
   a. Walking only on the designated path.
   b. Walking on the grass that borders the trail if the trail is very muddy.
   c. Taking a shortcut if you can find one because it means you will be walking less.
3. Why should you dispose of waste properly?
   a. You don't need to. Park rangers love to pick up the trash you leave behind.
   b. You should actually leave your leftovers behind, because animals will eat them. It is important to make sure they aren't hungry.
   c. So that other peoples' experiences of the park are not impacted by you leaving your waste behind.
4. How can you best follow the concept "leave what you find?"
   a. Take only a small rock or leaf to remember your trip.
   b. Take pictures, but leave any physical items where they are.
   c. Leave everything you find, unless it may be rare like an arrowhead, then it is okay to take.
5. What is not a good example of minimizing campfire impacts?
   a. Only having a campfire in a pre-existing campfire ring.
   b. Checking in with current conditions when you consider making a campfire.
   c. Building a new campfire ring in a location that has a better view.
6. What is a poor example of respecting wildlife?
   a. Building squirrel houses out of rocks so the squirrels have a place to live.
   b. Stay far away from wildlife and give them plenty of space.
   c. Reminding your grown-ups not to drive too fast in animal habitats while visiting the park.
7. How can you show consideration of other visitors?
   a. Play music on your speaker so other people at the campground can enjoy it.
   b. Wear headphones on the trail if you choose to listen to music.
   c. Make sure to yell "Hello!" to every animal you see at top volume.

Park Poetry

America's parks inspire art of all kinds. Painters, sculptors, photographers, writers, and artists of all mediums have taken inspiration from natural beauty. They have turned their inspiration into great works.

Use this space to write your own poem about the park. Think about what you have experienced or seen. Use descriptive language to create an acrostic poem. This type of poem has the first letter of each line spell out another word. Create an acrostic that spells out the word "Forest."

F _____

O _____

R _____

E _____

S _____

T _____

Fresh air

Open skies

Ready to

Explore

So many

Trees from ancient times

Family time

On our way

Relaxing

Everyone excited

Singing songs

Terrific memories

Staying Safe in the Sun

It is important to take precautions to stay safe outdoors, especially when it is very hot outside. When someone gets overheated or dehydrated, they may feel sick or even require medical attention.

Use the cryptogram below to decode three tips on how to prevent heat-related illnesses. You may need to do some math to figure out the answers.

T _ _ _   _ _ _ _ _ _   _ _ _   _ _ _ _
12 5 12/2 50   30 21 50 5 2x3 36   3x4 27   21 50 6x6 12

_ _   _ _ _   _ _ _ _ _ .
99 10   15-3 4 50   36 7-3 5 1 50

_ _ _ _   H _ _ _ _ _ _ _   _ _
36 12 1x5 18   4 2x9 1 21 5 12 50 8-7   30 18

_ _ _ _ _ _ _ _   _ _ _ _   _ _   _ _ _ _ _ .
1 21 99 10 6 33x3 10 75   35 3x9 12 36   27 5x5   18/2 5 12 50 21

_ _ A _   _ _ _ _ _ _ _ _ _   _ _ _
9 50 12-7 21   36 3 10 36 15 21 5x10 50 10   5 10 12-11

_ _ _   _ - _ _ _ _ _ _ _ _ _
36 3 10   8 7x3 27 12 50 15 9+3 99 80 50

_ _ _ _ _ _ _ I N G .
15 35 27 12 2x2 99 10 75

a	b	c	d	e	f	g	h	i	j	k	l	m	n	o
5	30	15	1	50	25	75	4	99	20	6	35	49	10	27

p	q	r	s	t	u	v	w	x	y	z
8	16	21	36	12	3	80	9	40	18	7

Get Your Kicks on Route 66

start here

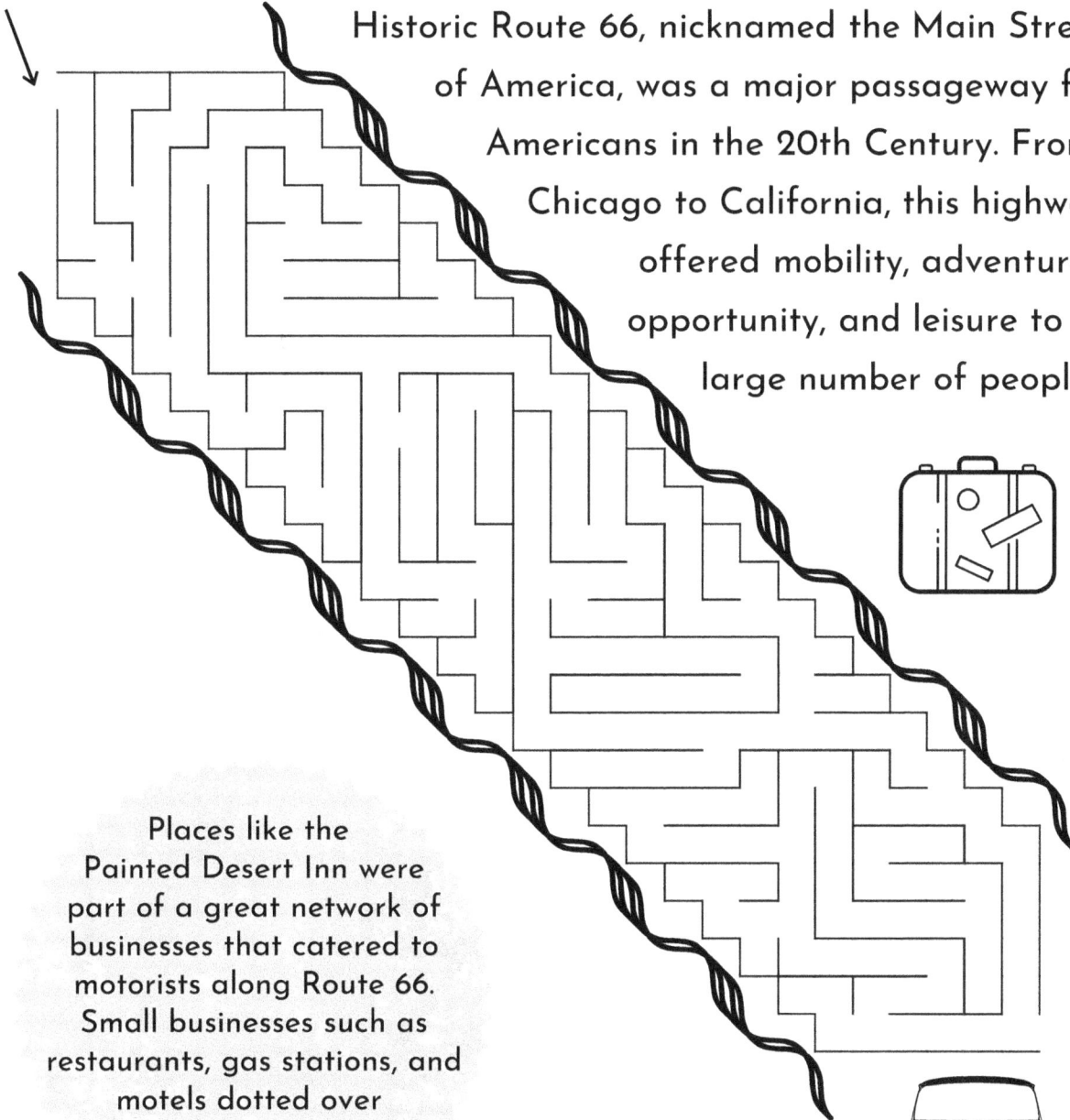

Historic Route 66, nicknamed the Main Street of America, was a major passageway for Americans in the 20th Century. From Chicago to California, this highway offered mobility, adventure, opportunity, and leisure to a large number of people.

Places like the Painted Desert Inn were part of a great network of businesses that catered to motorists along Route 66. Small businesses such as restaurants, gas stations, and motels dotted over 2,200 miles of the open road.

Stacking Rocks

Have you ever seen stacks of rocks while hiking in national parks? Do you know what they are or what they mean? These rock piles are called cairns and often mark hiking routes in parks. Every park has a different way to maintain trails and cairns. However, they all have the same rule: If you come across a cairn, do not disturb it!

Color the cairn and the rules to remember.

1. Do not tamper with cairns.

If a cairn is tampered with or an unauthorized one is built, then future visitors may become disoriented or even lost.

2. Do not build unauthorized cairns.

Moving rocks disturbs the soil and makes the area more prone to erosion. Disturbing rocks can disturb fragile plants.

3. Do not add to existing cairns.

Authorized cairns are carefully designed. Adding to them can actually cause them to collapse.

Decoding Using American Sign Language

American Sign Language, also called ASL for short, is a language that many Deaf people or people who are hard of hearing use to communicate. People use ASL to communicate with their hands. Did you know people from all over the country and world travel to national parks? You may hear people speaking other languages. You might also see people using ASL. Use the American Manual Alphabet chart to decode some national parks facts.

This was the first national park to be established:

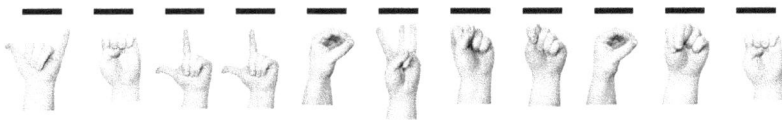

_ _ _ _ _ _ _ _ _ _ _

This is the biggest national park in the US:

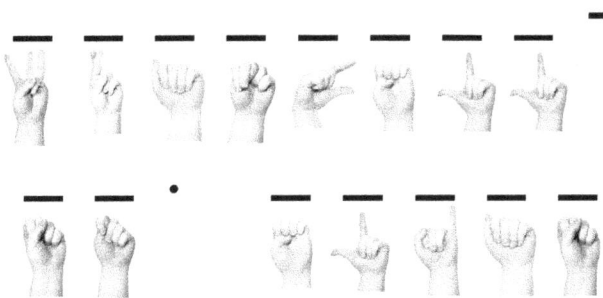

_ _ _ _ _ _ _ _ -

_ _ . _ _ _ _ _

This is the most visited national park:

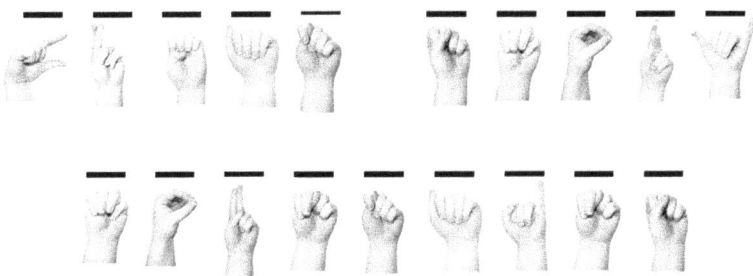

_ _ _ _ _ _ _ _ _

_ _ _ _ _ _ _ _

Aa	Bb	Cc	Dd	Ee
Ff	Gg		Hh	Ii
Jj	Kk	Ll	Mm	Nn
Oo	Pp		Qq	Rr
Ss	Tt		Uu	Vv
Ww	Xx		Yy	Zz

Hint: Pay close attention to the position of the thumb!

Try it! Using the chart, try to make the letters of the alphabet with your hand. What is the hardest letter to make? Can you spell out your name? Show a friend or family member and have them watch you spell out the name of the national park you are in.

Go Birdwatching Along the Rio Puerco

start here

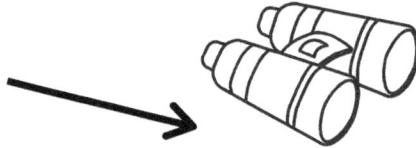

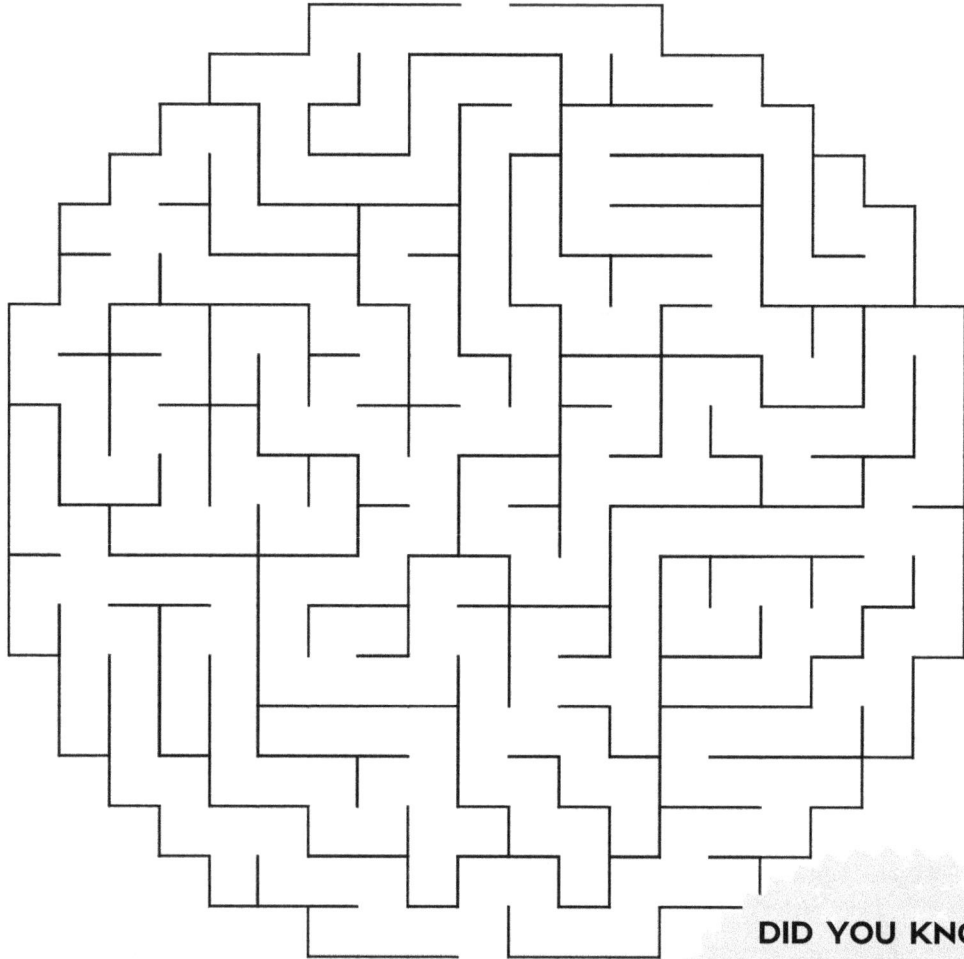

DID YOU KNOW?

Petrified Forest is home to both resident and migratory bird species. Migratory birds are ones that make seasonal movements, often flying long distances. Resident birds do not migrate and live in the same area year-round.

Butterflies of the Painted Desert

Dozens of species of butterflies and moths live in Petrified Forest National Park. Their wingspan size varies, as do the patterns on their wings. Design your own butterfly below. Make sure the wings are symmetrical, which means both sides match.

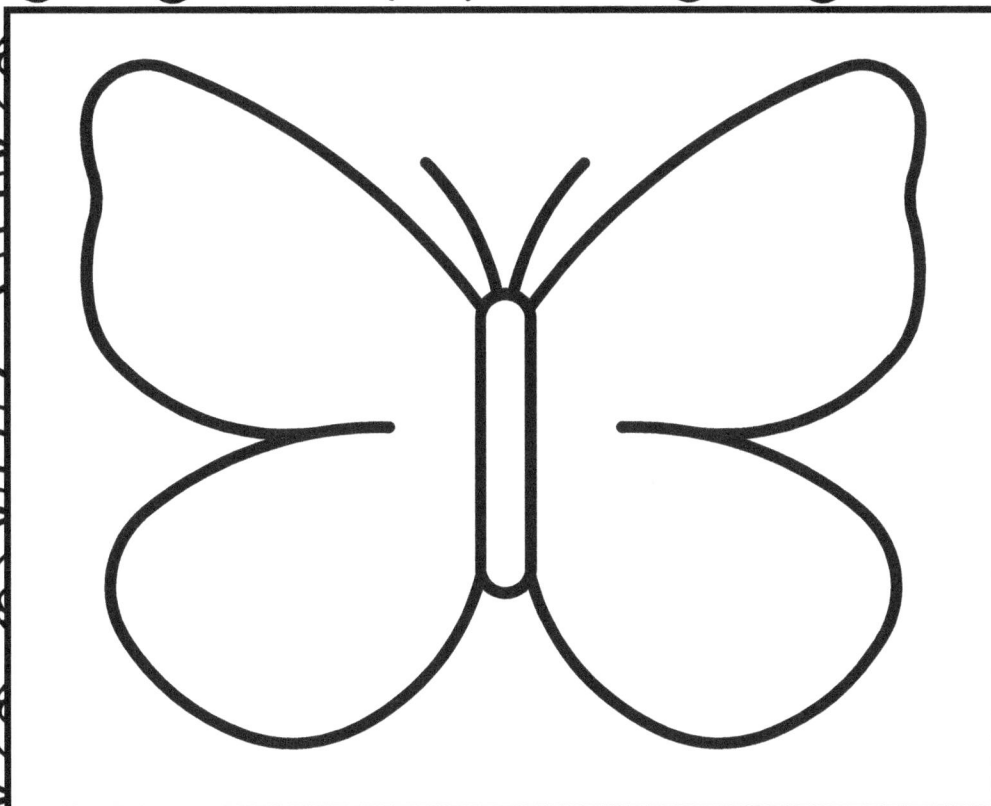

A Hike at Blue Mesa

Fill in the blanks on this page without looking at the full story. Once you have each line filled out, use the words you've chosen to complete the story on the next page.

ADJECTIVE _____

SOMETHING TO EAT _____

SOMETHING TO DRINK _____

NOUN _____

ARTICLE OF CLOTHING _____

BODY PART _____

VERB _____

ANIMAL _____

SAME TYPE OF FOOD _____

ADJECTIVE _____

SAME ANIMAL _____

VERB THAT ENDS IN "ED" _____

NUMBER _____

A DIFFERENT NUMBER _____

SOMETHING THAT FLIES _____

LIGHT SOURCE _____

PLURAL NOUN _____

FAMILY MEMBER _____

YOUR NICKNAME _____

A Hike at Blue Mesa

Use the words from the previous page to complete a silly story.

I went for a hike at Blue Mesa today. In my favorite _ _ _ _ _ _ _ backpack, I
ADJECTIVE

made sure to pack a map so I wouldn't get lost. I also threw in an extra

_ _ _ _ _ _ _ _ _ _ _ just in case I got hungry and a bottle of _ _ _ _ _ _ _ _ _ _ _. I put
SOMETHING TO EAT   SOMETHING TO DRINK

on my _ _ _ _ _ _ _ _ _ spray, and I tied a _ _ _ _ _ _ _ _ _ _ _ _ around my
NOUN   ARTICLE OF CLOTHING

_ _ _ _ _ _ _ _ _ _, in case it gets chilly. I started to _ _ _ _ _ _ down the path. As
BODY PART   VERB

soon as I turned the corner, I came face to face with a(n) _ _ _ _ _ _ _ _. I think
ANIMAL

it was as startled as I was! What should I do? I had to think fast! Should I

give it some of my _ _ _ _ _ _ _ _ _ _ _? No. I had to remember what the
SAME TYPE OF FOOD

_ _ _ _ _ _ _ ranger told me: "If you see one, back away slowly and try not to
ADJECTIVE

scare it." Soon enough, the _ away. The coast
SAME ANIMAL   VERB THAT ENDS IN ED

was clear. _ _ _ _ _ _ hours later, I finally reached the lookout. I felt like I could
NUMBER

see for a _ _ _ _ _ _ miles. I took a picture of a _ _ _ _ _ _ _ _ so I could always
A DIFFERENT NUMBER   NOUN

remember this moment. As I was putting my camera away, a _ _ _ _ _ _ _ _ _
SOMETHING THAT FLIES

flew by, reminding me that it was almost nighttime. I turned on my

_ _ _ _ _ _ _ _ _ _ and headed back. I could hear the _ _ _ _ _ _ _ _ _ _ singing their
LIGHT SOURCE   PLURAL INSECT

evening song. Just as I was getting tired, I saw my _ _ _ _ _ _ _ _ _ _ and our tent.
FAMILY MEMBER

"Welcome back _ _ _ _ _ _ _ _! How was your hike?"
NICKNAME

41

Hidden Picture

After a long day of summer hiking, you might find your way into the Painted Desert Inn in search of something like this.

2	2	2	2	2/4	4	4	2/4	2	2	2	2
2	2	2	2/4	4	4	4	4	2/4	2	2	2
2	2	2	2/4	6/6	6	4	4	4	4/2	2	2
2	2/6	6	6	6	4/6	4/7	7	7	7	2/7	2
2	2/6	6	6	6	6	6/7	7	7	7	7/2	2
2	9	9	9	9	9	9	9	9	9	9	2
2	8	8	8	8	8	8	8	8	8	8	2
2	2	9	9	9	9	9	9	9	9	2	2
2	2	9	9	9	9	9	9	9	9	2	2
2	2	2	2	2	9	9	2	2	2	2	2
2	2	2	2	2	9	9	2	2	2	2	2
2	2	2	2	9	9	9	9	2	2	2	2

Directions:

You will need crayons or colored pencils in each of the listed colors. Use the color code to help you figure out what the hidden picture is. For example, you will color every square with the number 8 dark blue. Some squares will call for more than one color.

2 - ORANGE
4 - PINK
6 - BROWN
7 - CREAM
8 - DARK BLUE
9 - LIGHT BLUE

Let's Go Camping in the Painted Desert

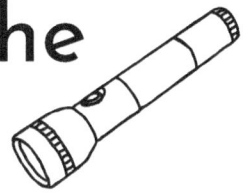

Words may be horizontal, vertical, diagonal, or they might even be backwards!

1. tent
2. camp stove
3. sleeping bag
4. bug spray
5. sunscreen
6. map
7. flashlight
8. pillow
9. lantern
10. ice
11. snacks
12. smores
13. water
14. first aid kit
15. chair
16. cards
17. books
18. games
19. trail
20. hat

```
D P P I L L O W D B T E A C I
E O A D P R E A A M B R C A N
P W C A M P S T O V E I H X G
R A H S G E L E B E E D A P S
E L B U G S P R A Y N G I E A
S I A H G C I C N N M E R C N
C W N L A F I R S K O O B F K
M T A E M I L E L H M R W L J
T A P R E A O R E S L B A A B
S M P A S R R T E N T L U S C
C E A I I R C G P E I U J H A
S S N A C K S S I M O K I L R
I J R S F O I S N J R A Q I D
C Y E T L E V E G U O R V G S
E W T A K C A B B S S O H H M
X J N F I R S T A I D K I T T
U A A E S S E N G E T P V A B
C J L I A R T D N A M A H A S
```

All in the Day of a Park Ranger

Park Rangers are hardworking individuals dedicated to protecting our parks, monuments, museums, and more. They take care of the natural and cultural resources for future generations. Rangers also help protect the visitors of the park. Their responsibilities are broad and they work both with the public and behind the scenes.

What have you seen park rangers do? Use your knowledge of the duties of park rangers to fill out a typical daily schedule, listing one activity for each hour. Feel free to make up your own, but some examples of activities are provided on the right. Read carefully! Not all the example activities are befitting a ranger.

Time	Activity		Examples
6 am	Lead a sunrise hike		• feed the migratory birds
7 am			• build trails for visitors to enjoy
8 am			• throw rocks off the side of the hill
9 am			• rescue lost hikers
10 am			• study animal behavior
11 am			• record air quality data
12 pm	Enjoy a lunch break outside		• answer questions at the visitor center
1 pm			• pick wildflowers
2 pm			• pick up litter
3 pm			• share marshmallows with squirrels
4 pm	Teach visitors about the geology of the desert		• repair handrails
5 pm			• lead a class on a field trip
6 pm			• catch toads and make them race
7 pm			• lead people on educational hikes
8 pm			• write articles for the park website
9 pm			• protect the river from pollution

Additional examples:
- remove non-native plants from the park
- study how climate change is affecting the park
- give a talk about mountain lions
- lead a program for campers on pronghorn

If you were a park ranger, which of the above tasks would you enjoy most?

_____

_____

Draw Yourself as a Park Ranger

RANGER

Map Symbol Sudoku

The National Park System makes park maps using symbols instead of words.
They are easily understood and take up way less space on a tiny map.

Trailhead	Cabin	Wildlife	Campground

Complete this symbol sudoku puzzle. Fill each square with one of the symbols. Each one can appear only once in each row, column, and mini 2x2 grid. Each symbol means something, so you can write what the symbol represents instead of drawing the symbols if you prefer.

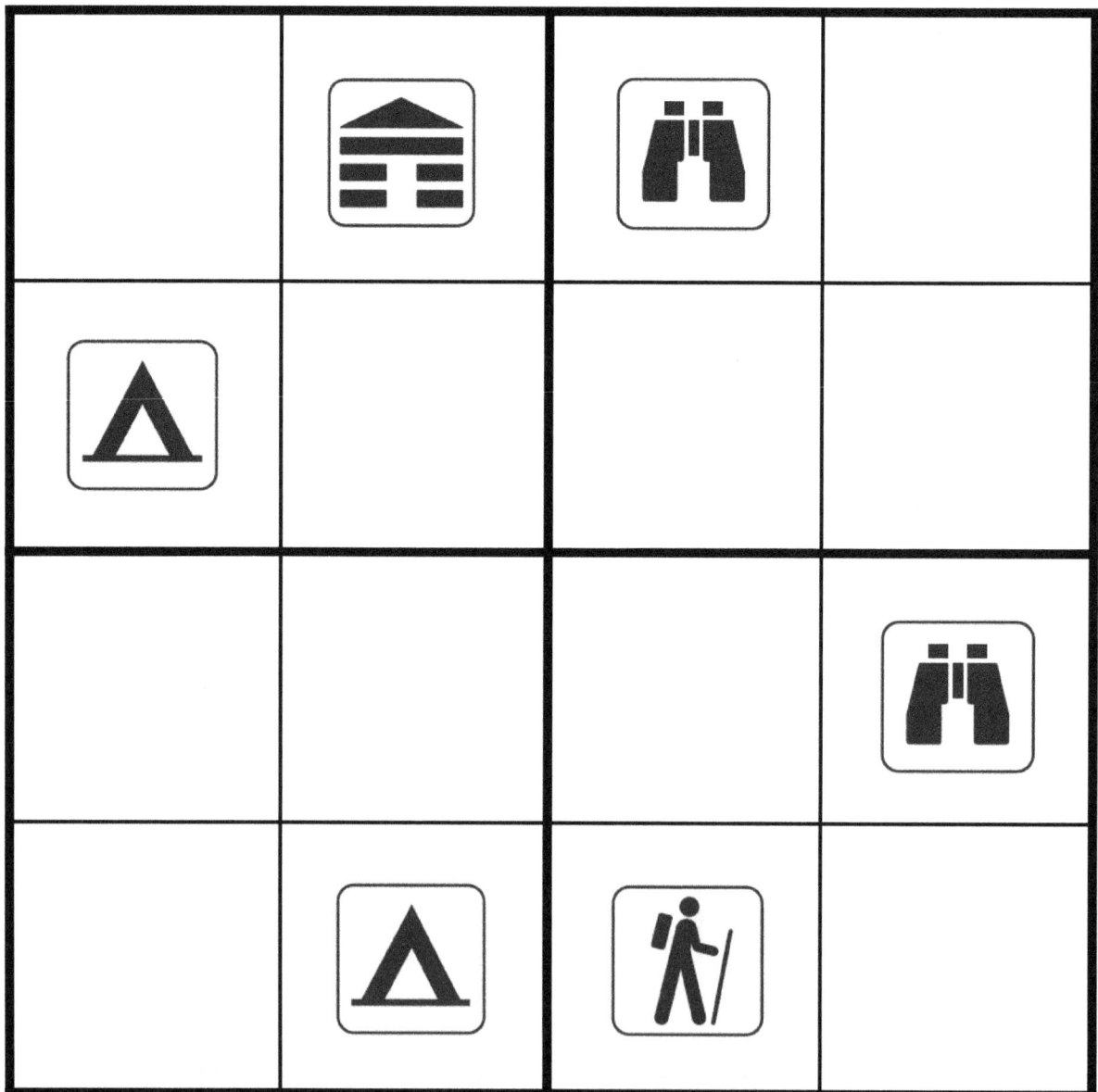

	Cabin	Wildlife	
Campground			
			Wildlife
	Campground	Trailhead	

Geocaching

Geocaching, pronounced "geo-cashing," is a worldwide treasure hunt. Participants use GPS (Global Positioning System) devices such as smartphones to locate a hidden "cache." Caches may be physical objects like containers or they may be virtual. Searching for a cache is like going on a treasure hunt! It can involve clues, riddles, and visits to multiple locations.

Petrified Forest National Park is one of the many parks that have created geocaches for visitors to search for and find. Some caches are only small enough for a logbook, but some are containers with small items you can trade, such as toys, keychains, stickers, and other trinkets.

Do you keep a box of treasured items at home?
Draw some trinkets you would like to find in a geocache!

Create a PSA for Petrified Forest National Park

One job of the National Park Service is to protect and preserve park resources both for today and for future generations. These park resources are different depending on where you go. Sometimes this can mean endangered plants or animals, other times it can mean cultural artifacts. In Petrified Forest National Park, the petrified wood and other fossils are park resources that require protection.

A public service announcement (PSA) is a tool used to educate people and persuade them to act a certain way. PSAs are not designed to sell something. Instead benefit the public, usually with health or safety in mind.

Create a PSA for kids your age. Your PSA should persuade kids not to move or take pieces of petrified wood or fossils from the park. It is important not to move these objects because it takes away the context. Context refers to where and how fossils or artifacts are found and described. Context is as important as the objects themselves. It is important not to remove these objects so that future visitors to the park also have the chance to experience seeing them. It also ensures future research can be done by park scientists.

Can you think of an example PSA you are familiar with?

_____

_____

What is the message of that PSA? What is it promoting?

_____

_____

Do you think it is a persuasive PSA?

_____

_____

On the next page, design a poster for your PSA. If you need to learn more about the issue of people taking objects from the park, you can ask a park ranger. If you are not able to visit the park in person, have a grown-up help you call or email a ranger.

Your PSA should:
☐ Include a clear message
☐ Have a catchy slogan
☐ Be designed for a specific audience
☐ Have a picture that reflects the message
☐ Include persuasive information

Create your PSA poster here

63 National Parks

How many other national parks have you been to? Which one do you want to visit next? Note that if some of these parks fall on the border of more than one state, you may check it off more than once!

Alaska
- [ ] Denali National Park
- [ ] Gates of the Arctic National Park
- [ ] Glacier Bay National Park
- [ ] Katmai National Park
- [ ] Kenai Fjords National Park
- [ ] Kobuk Valley National Park
- [ ] Lake Clark National Park
- [ ] Wrangell-St. Elias National Park

American Samoa
- [ ] National Park of American Samoa

Arizona
- [ ] Grand Canyon National Park
- [ ] Petrified Forest National Park
- [ ] Saguaro National Park

Arkansas
- [ ] Hot Springs National Park

California
- [ ] Channel Islands National Park
- [ ] Death Valley National Park
- [ ] Joshua Tree National Park
- [ ] Kings Canyon National Park
- [ ] Lassen Volcanic National Park
- [ ] Pinnacles National Park
- [ ] Redwood National Park
- [ ] Sequoia National Park
- [ ] Yosemite National Park

Colorado
- [ ] Black Canyon of the Gunnison National Park
- [ ] Great Sand Dunes National Park
- [ ] Mesa Verde National Park
- [ ] Rocky Mountain National Park

Florida
- [ ] Biscayne National Park
- [ ] Dry Tortugas National Park
- [ ] Everglades National Park

Hawaii
- [ ] Haleakalā National Park
- [ ] Hawai'i Volcanoes National Park

Idaho
- [ ] Yellowstone National Park

Kentucky
- [ ] Mammoth Cave National Park

Indiana
- [ ] Indiana Dunes National Park

Maine
- [ ] Acadia National Park

Michigan
- [ ] Isle Royale National Park

Minnesota
- [ ] Voyageurs National Park

Missouri
- [ ] Gateway Arch National Park

Montana
- [ ] Glacier National Park
- [ ] Yellowstone National Park

Nevada
- [ ] Death Valley National Park
- [ ] Great Basin National Park

New Mexico
- [ ] Carlsbad Caverns National Park
- [ ] White Sands National Park

North Dakota
- [ ] Theodore Roosevelt National Park

North Carolina
- [ ] Great Smoky Mountains National Park

Ohio
- [ ] Cuyahoga Valley National Park

Oregon
- [ ] Crater Lake National Park

South Carolina
- [ ] Congaree National Park

South Dakota
- [ ] Badlands National Park
- [ ] Wind Cave National Park

Tennessee
- [ ] Great Smoky Mountains National Park

Texas
- [ ] Big Bend National Park
- [ ] Guadalupe Mountains National Park

Utah
- [ ] Arches National Park
- [ ] Bryce Canyon National Park
- [ ] Canyonlands National Park
- [ ] Capitol Reef National Park
- [ ] Zion National Park

Virgin Islands
- [ ] Virgin Islands National Park

Virginia
- [ ] Shenandoah National Park

Washington
- [ ] Mount Rainier National Park
- [ ] North Cascades National Park
- [ ] Olympic National Park

West Virginia
- [ ] New River Gorge National Park

Wyoming
- [ ] Grand Teton National Park
- [ ] Yellowstone National Park

Other National Parks Crossword

Besides Petrified Forest National Park, there are 62 other diverse and beautiful national parks across the United States. Try your hand at this crossword. If you need help, look at the previous page for some hints.

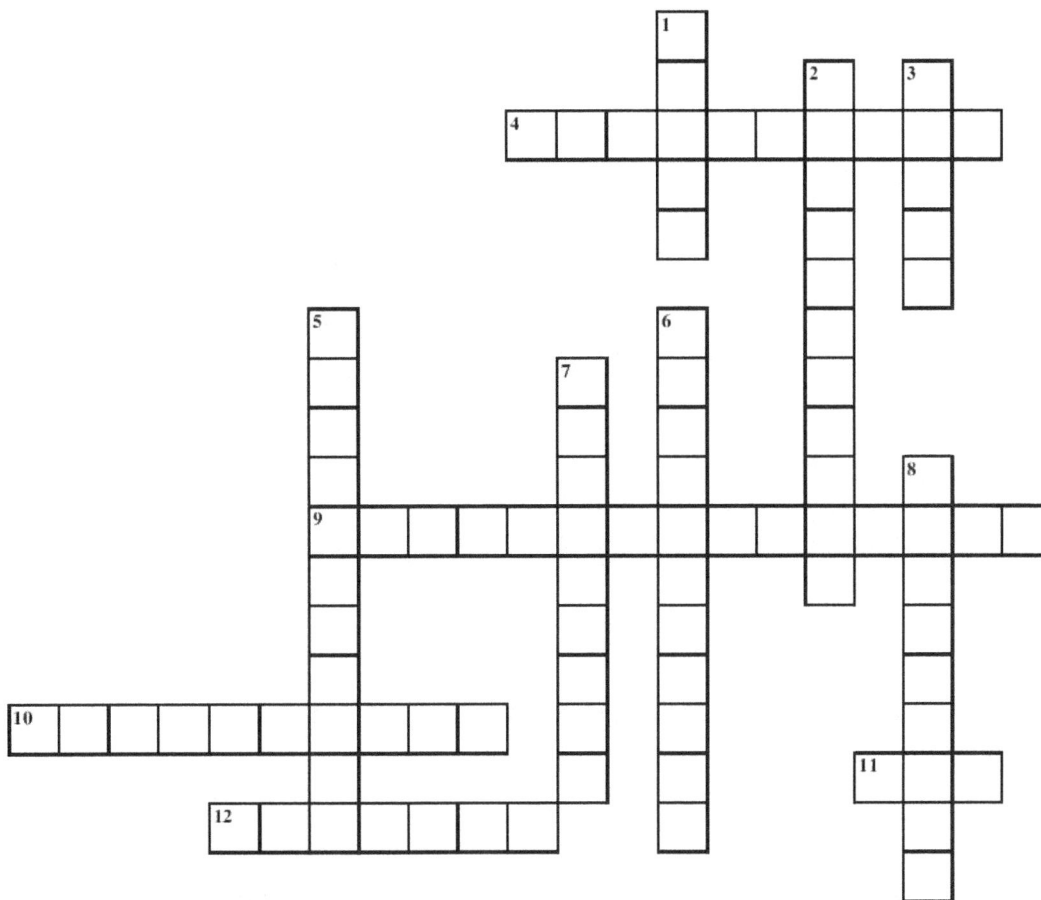

Down

1. State where Acadia National Park is located
2. This national park has the Spanish word for turtle in it
3. Number of national parks in Alaska
5. This national park has some of the hottest temperatures in the world
6. This national park is the only one in Idaho
7. This toothsome creature can famously be found in Everglades National Park
8. Only president with a national park named for them

Across

4. This state has the most national parks.
9. This park has some of the newest land in the US, caused by volcanic eruptions.
10. This park has the deepest lake in the United States.
11. This color shows up in the name of a national park in California.
12. This national park deserves a gold medal.

Which National Park Will You Go To Next?
Word Search

1. Zion
2. Big Bend
3. Glacier
4. Olympic
5. Sequoia
6. Bryce
7. Mesa Verde
8. Biscayne
9. Wind Cave
10. Great Basin
11. Katmai
12. Yellowstone
13. Voyageurs
14. Arches
15. Badlands
16. Denali
17. Glacier Bay
18. Hot Springs

```
F M M E S A V E R D E B N E Y
E A B I G B E N D E S A S E M
Y L I C A L O Y N E E D L T G
D M G A S S A U C N R L U E R
C E L I I T S C R E O A A K E
S N A W Y E E O I W T N A C A
G I C H A A Q C S E M D N S T
N O I Z P R U T I M R S N E B
I W E L M P O N B W E B K H A
R J R F D N I F L I H B U C S
P A B E E S A N E S O P W R I
S J A E N Y A C S I B A U A N
T C Y I A D O H H Y M E A L R
O T A T L M L E S E G R W R J
H S T O I K A T M A I R O P B
I C H U R C O L Y M P I C O U
O Y G T S D E O S B R Y C E T
W I N D C A V E I N R O H E M
```

Field Notes

Spend some time reflecting on your trip to Petrified Forest National Park. Your field notes will help you remember the things you experienced. Use the space below to write about your day.

While I was at Petrified Forest National Park...

I saw:

_____

_____

_____

_____

I heard:

_____

_____

_____

I felt:

_____

_____

Draw a picture of your favorite thing in the park.

I wondered:

_____

_____

_____

_____

_____

ANSWER KEY

Go Horseback Riding in the Painted Desert

Help find the horse's lost shoe!

start here →

DID YOU KNOW?

Horseback riding is a popular activity in Petrified Forest National Park. You can take horses for day or overnight trips in the Painted Desert Wilderness Area.

Answers: Who Lives in Petrified Forest?

Below are 7 plants and animals that live in the park. Use the word bank to fill in the clues below. Pay attention to how many letters each word has to see where it fits.

BOBC A T

BURROG R ASS

K I T ■ FOX

BUZ Z ARD

COTT O NWOOD

PRO N GHORN

S A LAMANDER

WORD BANK: COTTONWOOD, PRONGHORN, SALAMANDER, BOBCAT, BURROGRASS, KIT FOX, BUZZARD

56

Find the Match!
Common Names and Latin Names

Match the common name to the scientific name for each animal. The first one is done for you. Use clues on the page before and after this one to complete the matches.

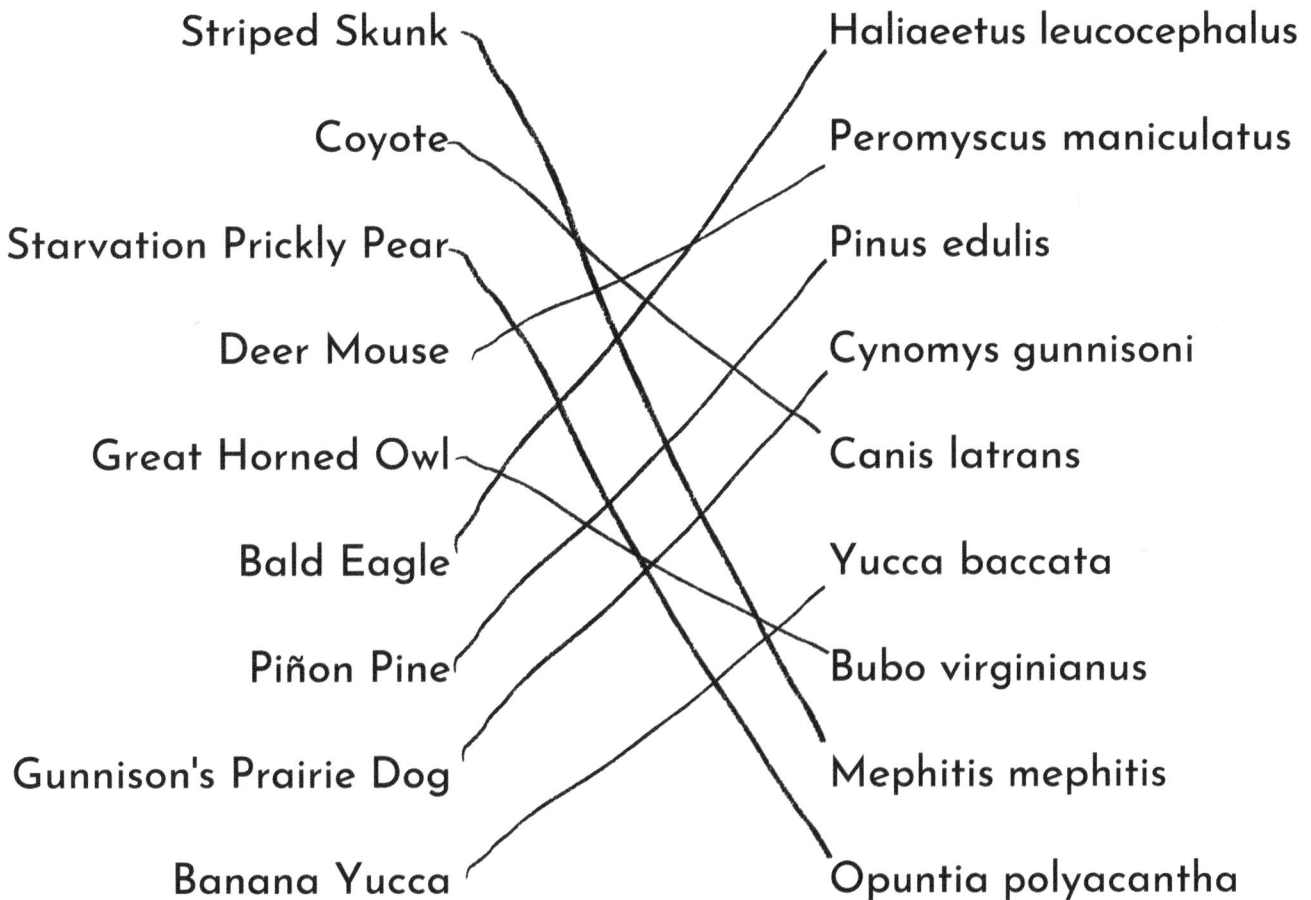

Striped Skunk   Haliaeetus leucocephalus

Coyote   Peromyscus maniculatus

Starvation Prickly Pear   Pinus edulis

Deer Mouse   Cynomys gunnisoni

Great Horned Owl   Canis latrans

Bald Eagle   Yucca baccata

Piñon Pine   Bubo virginianus

Gunnison's Prairie Dog   Mephitis mephitis

Banana Yucca   Opuntia polyacantha

Bald Eagle

Haliaeetus leucocephalus

Jumbles Answers

1. GEOCACHING

2. HIKING

3. BIRDING

4. CAMPING

5. PICNICKING

6. SIGHTSEEING

7. STAR GAZING

National Park Emblem Answers

1. This represents all plants: **Sequoia Tree**

2. This represents all animals: **Bison**

3. This represents the landscapes: **Mountains**

4. This represents the waters protected by the park service: **Water**

5. This represents the historical and archeological values: **Arrowhead**

Answers: The Ten Essentials

Careful preparation and knowledge are key to a successful adventure into Petrified Forest's backcountry.

The ten essentials are a list of things that are important to have when you go for longer hikes. If you go on a hike to the <u>backcountry,</u> it is especially important that you have everything you need in case of an emergency. If you get lost or something unforeseen happens, it is good to be prepared to survive until help finds you.

The ten essentials list was developed in the 1930s by an outdoors group called the Mountaineers. Over time and technological advancements, this list has evolved. Can you identify all the things on the current list? Circle each of the "essentials" and cross out everything that doesn't make the cut.

(fire: matches, lighter, tinder, and/or stove)	~~a pint of milk~~	~~extra money~~	(headlamp, plus extra batteries)	(extra clothes)
(extra water)	~~a dog~~	~~Polaroid camera~~	~~bug net~~	~~lightweight games like a deck of cards~~
(extra food)	~~a roll of duct tape~~	(shelter)	(sun protection, such as sunglasses, sun-protective clothes and sunscreen)	(knife, plus a gear repair kit)
~~a mirror~~	(navigation: map, compass, altimeter, GPS device, or satellite messenger)	(first aid kit)	~~extra flip-flops~~	~~entertainment like video games or books~~

Backcountry - a remote undeveloped rural area.

Petrified Forest Word Search

Words may be horizontal, vertical, or diagonal
and they might be backward!

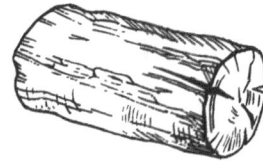

1. TREES
2. BADLANDS
3. PUERCO
4. PUEBLO
5. LONG LOGS
6. PALEONTOLOGY
7. PAINTED
8. HOPI
9. ZUNI
10. NAVAJO
11. TIME
12. BASKETMAKER
13. HOLBROOK
14. PETRIFIED
15. ARIZONA
16. FOSSIL
17. AGATE HOUSE

```
C W P A L E O N T O L O G Y K
H T U P K I A I C R E L A N P
T G E O U O M R C C E B A R E
P M R A Y E R S I E R L I E T
I I C D R A B L O Z I P I K R
N F O S S I L L D C O T K A I
Y E S E E H E K O H P N I M F
S G O L G N O L G E N E A T I
N E H B S D T O R E C D G E E
E C I C A D T U S H P I O K D
I K A P A I N T E D K E T S N
N R O A K O E A O V O K I A E
E I P O T Z D E L E R T L B W
J C G F R O U E P D O R V E H
Z I L S E B I N A V A J O E A
U T A I E E L G E Z E B R N L
N T D T S E N O Y N A C C I E
I J U O E S U O H E T A G A Z
```

60

Wildlife Wisdom

The national park is home to many different kinds of animals. Seeing wildlife can be an exciting part of visiting the national park but it is important to remember that these animals are wild. They need plenty of space and a healthy habitat where they can find their own food. Part of this is not allowing animals to eat any human food. This is their home and we are the visitors. We need to be respectful of the wildlife in the park.

Directions: Circle the highlighted words that best complete the following sentences.

If an animal changes its behavior because of your presence, you are:
A) too close
B) funny looking
C) dehydrated and should drink more water

The best thing we can do to help wild animals survive is:
A) make them pets
B) protect their habitat
C) knit them winter sweaters

In a national park, it is okay to share your food with wild animals:
A) never
B) always
C) sometimes

When you're hiking in an area where there are bears, you should warn bears that you are entering their space by:
A) hiking quietly
B) making noise
C) wearing bright colors

At night, park rangers care for the animals by:
A) putting them back into their cages
B) tucking them into bed
C) leaving them alone

If you see an abandoned bird's nest, it is best to:
A) pet the baby birds
B) leave it alone
C) crunch the empty eggshells

Bears look under logs in hopes of finding:
A) granola bars
B) leaves, stems, and seeds
C) peanuts to eat

The place where an animal lives is called its:
A) condo
B) habitat
C) crib

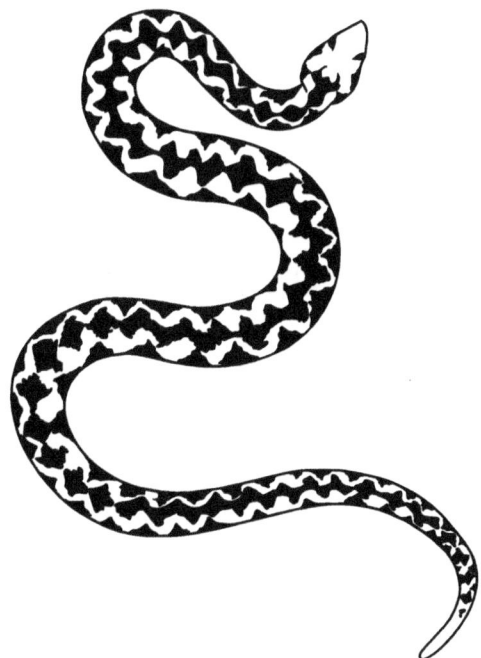

61

Hike to Hoodoos

DID YOU KNOW?
There are hoodoos at Devil's Playground within the park. Hoodoos are rock formations shaped by erosion.

Painted Desert Inn
Word Search

Once a place to rest for travelers on Route 66, the Painted Desert Inn is now a museum. If you visit the building today, you can learn about its history and see where tourists would eat, sleep, and admire the landscape of this area.

1. TREEHOUSE
2. LODGING
3. LORE
4. TOURIST
5. ROOM
6. CLAY
7. PUEBLO
8. STUCCO
9. STRUCTURE
10. HISTORIC
11. SOUVENIR
12. KABOTIE
13. MURAL
14. COLTER
15. LANDMARK
16. ICE CREAM
17. FLAGSTONE

```
P K A B O T I E A Y I D E O W
G N I G D O L M A T I O N R O
T V D T C U L E L W A L K O T
S E U C S R E G A O T T B M H
G E U L O I O C R E R R S K M
M T D L Y S R O U R E E L O A
S O S E H T C R M O E R L E E
A R B S I K I B D I H T O M R
L S A O S I L O E O O D L P C
L L I D T R K N K E U G B O E
F K A C O T I I N L S B E O C
S R L S R A O C S A E K U R I
T A O T I H I N Z I I L P E C
Y M A R C O O W K C O R D E B
R D R A S T R U C T U R E E M
T N E W G R E E E L B R T M T
L A D G E R I N E V U O S E B
F L A G S T O N E H Y S G O N
```

63

Answers: Leave No Trace Quiz

1. How can you plan ahead and prepare to ensure you have the best experience you can in the National Park?

    A. Make sure you stop by the ranger station for a map and to ask about current conditions.

2. What is an example of traveling on a durable surface?

    A. Walking only on the designated path.

3. Why should you dispose of waste properly?

    C. So that other peoples' experiences of the park are not impacted by you leaving your waste behind.

4. How can you best follow the concept "leave what you find?"

    B. Take pictures but leave any physical items where they are.

5. What is not a good example of minimizing campfire impacts?

    C. Building a new campfire ring in a location that has a better view.

6. What is a poor example of respecting wildlife?

    A. Building squirrel houses out of rocks from the river so the squirrels have a place to live.

7. How can you show consideration of other visitors?

    B. Wear headphones on the trail if you choose to listen to music.

Staying Safe in the Sun

Take breaks to rest in the shade.

Stay hydrated by drinking lots of water.

Wear sunscreen and sun-protective clothing.

Get Your Kicks on Route 66

ROUTE 66

start here

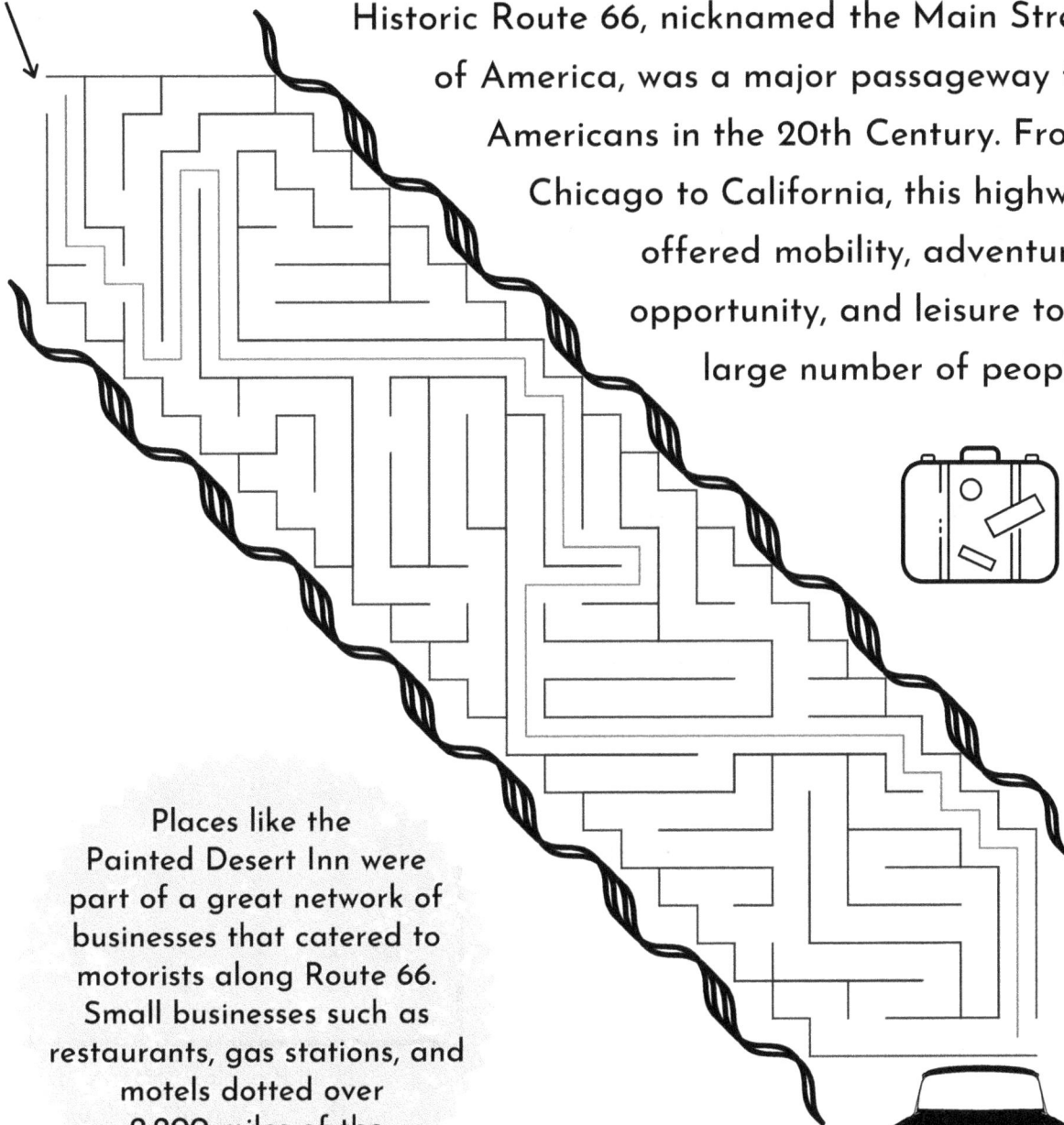

Historic Route 66, nicknamed the Main Street of America, was a major passageway for Americans in the 20th Century. From Chicago to California, this highway offered mobility, adventure, opportunity, and leisure to a large number of people.

Places like the Painted Desert Inn were part of a great network of businesses that catered to motorists along Route 66. Small businesses such as restaurants, gas stations, and motels dotted over 2,200 miles of the open road.

Decoding Using American Sign Language

American Sign Language, also called ASL for short, is a language that many Deaf people or people who are hard of hearing use to communicate. People use ASL to communicate with their hands. Did you know people from all over the country and world travel to national parks? You may hear people speaking other languages. You might also see people using ASL. Use the American Manual Alphabet chart to decode some national parks facts.

This was the first national park to be established:

Y E L L O W S T O N E

This is the biggest national park in the US:

W R A N G E L L -

S T .   E L I A S

This is the most visited national park:

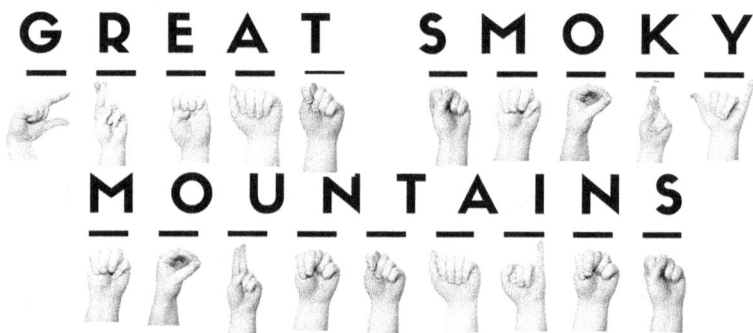

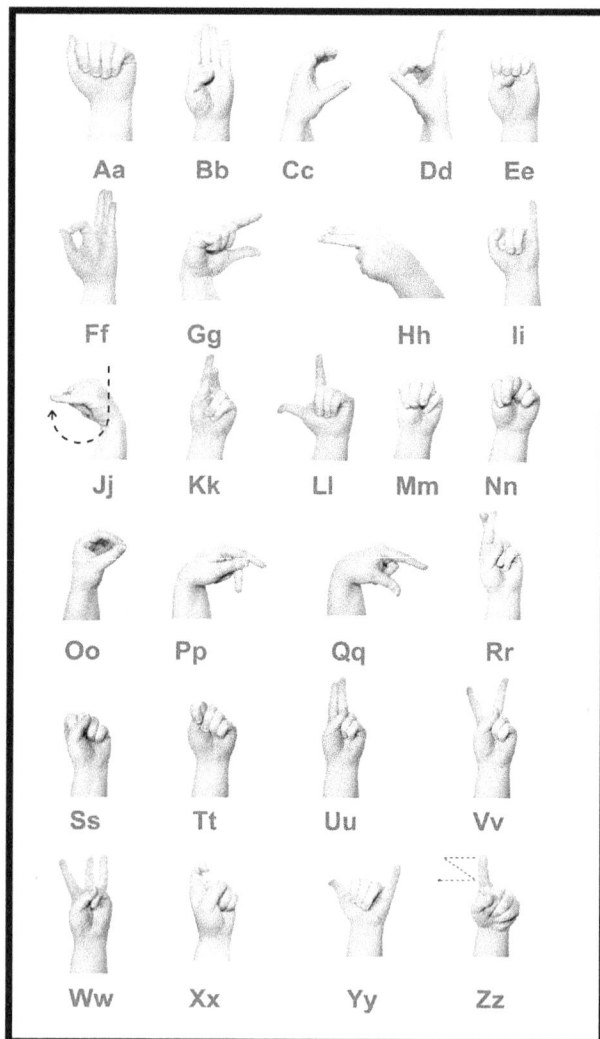

G R E A T   S M O K Y

M O U N T A I N S

Aa	Bb	Cc	Dd	Ee
Ff	Gg		Hh	Ii
Jj	Kk	Ll	Mm	Nn
Oo	Pp	Qq		Rr
Ss	Tt	Uu		Vv
Ww	Xx	Yy	Zz	

Hint: Pay close attention to the position of the thumb!

Try it! Using the chart, try to make the letters of the alphabet with your hand. What is the hardest letter to make? Can you spell out your name? Show a friend or family member and have them watch you spell out the name of the national park you are in.

Go Birdwatching Along the Rio Puerco

start here

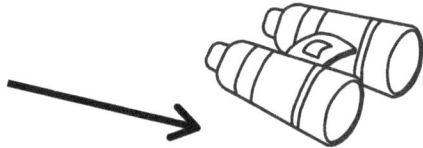

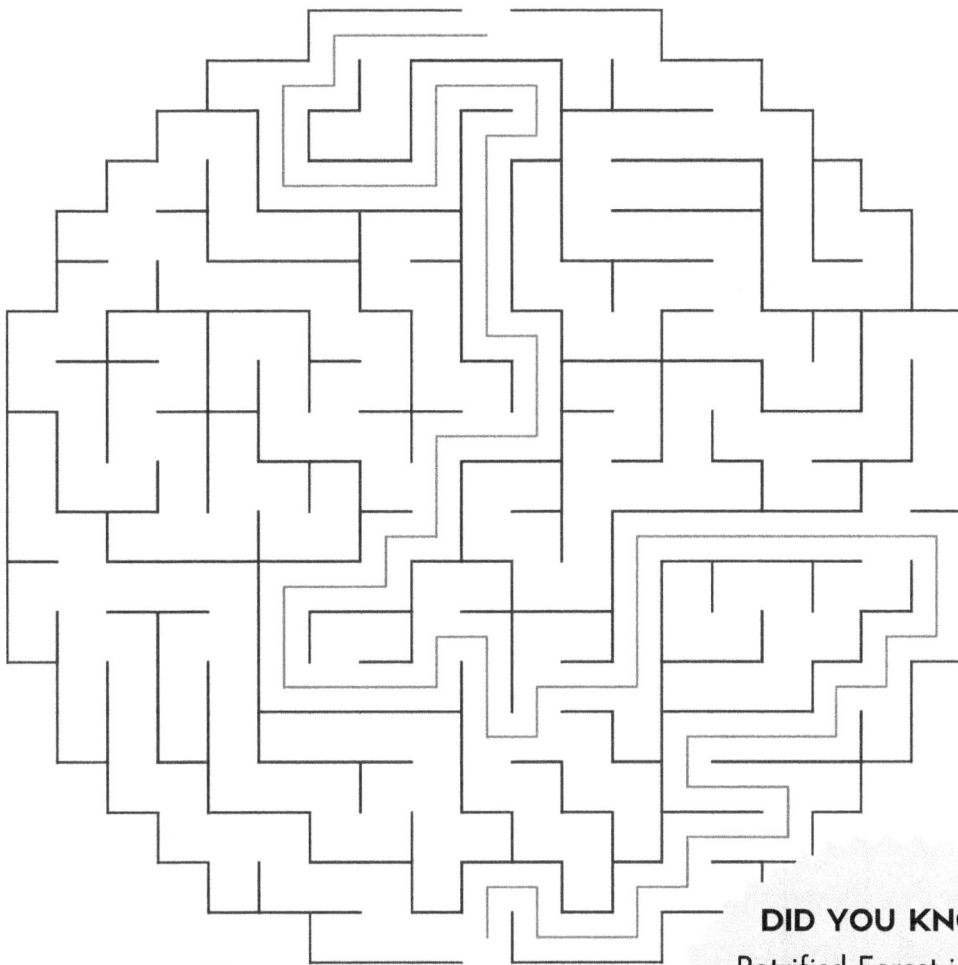

DID YOU KNOW?

Petrified Forest is home to both resident and migratory bird species. Migratory birds are ones that make seasonal movements, often flying long distances. Resident birds do not migrate and live in the same area year-round.

Let's Go Camping in the Painted Desert

1. tent
2. camp stove
3. sleeping bag
4. bug spray
5. sunscreen
6. map
7. flashlight
8. pillow
9. lantern
10. ice
11. snacks
12. smores
13. water
14. first aid kit
15. chair
16. cards
17. books
18. games
19. trail
20. hat

```
D P P I L L O W D B T E A C I
E O A D P R E A A M B R C A N
P W C A M P S T O V E I H X G
R A H S G E L E B E E D A P S
E L B U G S P R A Y N G I E A
S I A H G C I C N N M E R C N
C W N L A F I R S K O O B F K
M T A E M I L E L H M R W L J
T A P R E A O R E S L B A A B
S M P A S R R T E N T L U S C
C E A I I R C G P E I U J H A
S S N A C K S S I M O K I L R
I J R S F O I S N J R A Q I D
C Y E T L E V E G U O R V G S
E W T A K C A B B S S O H H M
X J N F I R S T A I D K I T T
U A A E S S E N G E T P V A B
C J L I A R T D N A M A H A S
```

68

All in the Day of a Park Ranger

There are many right answers for this activity, but not all of the provided examples are good activities for a park ranger. In fact, a park ranger's job may include stopping visitors from doing some of these things.

The list below are activities that rangers do not do:

feed the migratory birds

throw rocks off the side of the hill

pick wildflowers

share marshmallows with squirrels

catch toads and make them race

Map Symbol Sudoku Anwers

Answers: Other National Parks Crossword

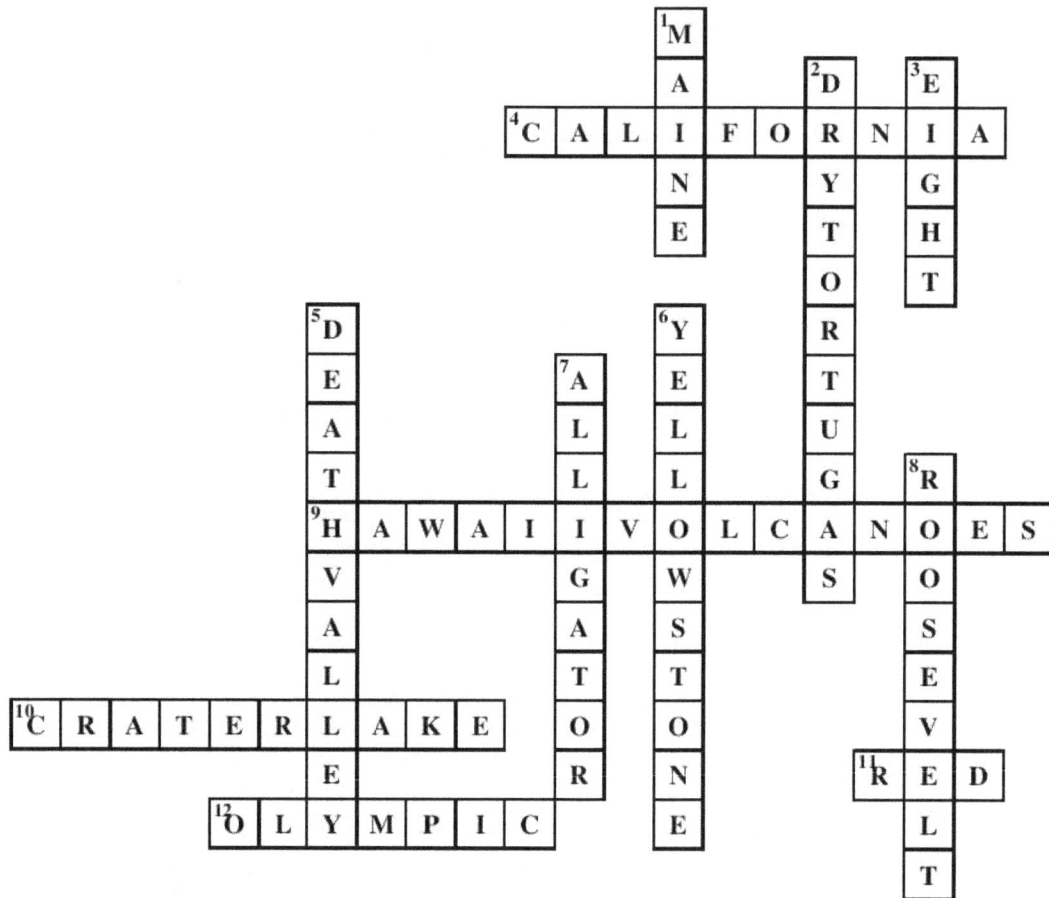

```
                              ¹M
                              A            ²D        ³E
        ⁴C  A  L  I  F  O  R  N  I  A
                              N           Y         G
                              E           T         H
                                          O         T
        ⁵D                    ⁶Y           R
        E              ⁷A     E           T
        A              L      L           U
        T              L      L           G        ⁸R
        ⁹H  A  W  A  I  I  V  O  L  C  A  N  O  E  S
        V              G      W           S        O
        A              A      S                    S
        L              T      T                    E
        ¹⁰C  R  A  T  E  R  L  A  K  E                 V
        E              O      O                    ¹¹R  E  D
        ¹²O  L  Y  M  P  I  C  N                      L
                       R      E                    T
```

Down

1. State where Acadia National Park is located
2. This National Park has the Spanish word for turtle in it
3. Number of National Parks in Alaska
5. This National Park has some of the hottest temperatures in the world
6. This National Park is the only one in Idaho
7. This toothsome creature can famously be found in Everglades National Park
8. Only president with a national park named for them

Across

4. This state has the most National Parks
9. This park has some of the newest land in the US, caused by a volcanic eruption
10. This park has the deepest lake in the United States
11. This color shows up in the name of a National Park in California
12. This National Park deserves a gold medal

Answers: Which National Park Will You Go To Next?

1. Zion
2. Big Bend
3. Glacier
4. Olympic
5. Sequoia
6. Bryce
7. Mesa Verde
8. Biscayne
9. Wind Cave
10. Great Basin
11. Katmai
12. Yellowstone
13. Voyageurs
14. Arches
15. Badlands
16. Denali
17. Glacier Bay
18. Hot Springs

F M M E S A V E R D E B N E Y
E A B I G B E N D E S A S E M
Y L I C A L O Y N E E D L T G
D M G A S S A U C N R L U E R
C E L I I T S C R E O A A K E
S N A W Y E E O I W T N A C A
G I C H A A Q C S E M D N S T
N O I Z P R U T I M R S N E B
I W E L M P O N B W E B K H A
R J R F D N I F L I H B U C S
P A B E E S A N E S O P W R I
S J A E N Y A C S I B A U A N
T C Y I A D O H H Y M E A L R
O T A T L M L E S E G R W R J
H S T O I K A T M A I R O P B
  I C H U R C O L Y M P I C O U
  O Y G T S D E O S B R Y C E T
W I N D C A V E I N R O H E M

LITTLE BISON

Press

Little Bison Press is an independent children's book publisher based in the Pacific Northwest. We promote exploration, conservation, and adventure through our books. Established in 2021, our passion for outside spaces and travel inspired the creation of Little Bison Press.

We seek to publish books that support children in learning about and caring for the natural places in our world.

To learn more, visit:
www.littlebisonpress.com

Want more free games and activities? Visit our website!